DIFFERENTIATING INSTRUCTION FOR DIVERSE LEARNERS

STRATEGIES FOR MEETING INDIVIDUAL NEEDS

By

MUJAHID BAKHT

1

DIFFERENTIATING INSTRUCTION FOR DIVERSE LEARNERS

STRATEGIES FOR MEETING INDIVIDUAL NEEDS

By:
MUJAHID BAKHT

Hardcover   ISBN 978-1-961299-02-3
Paperback   ISBN 978-1-961299-03-0
EBook   ISBN 978-1-961299-04-7

Published by:
Atlas Amazon, LLC.
United States of America.

The purpose of the book "Differentiating Instruction for Diverse Learners: Strategies for Meeting Individual Needs" by Mujhid Bakht is to provide educators with practical strategies and tools for effectively meeting the diverse learning needs of students in their classrooms. The book aims to help teachers create a learning environment that is responsive to the unique strengths and challenges of each student, allowing them to achieve their full potential.

Through this book, the author emphasizes the importance of recognizing and addressing the different learning styles, abilities, and needs of students, including English Language Learners, students with disabilities, and gifted and talented learners. The book provides educators with a range of differentiated instructional strategies and resources, including technology tools, collaborative learning activities, and assessment techniques that can be used to create an inclusive and engaging learning experience for all students.

The author also acknowledges the ongoing challenges and obstacles faced by educators in implementing differentiated instruction, and offers practical advice and guidance for overcoming resistance to change and addressing communication barriers in collaboration. The book emphasizes the importance of ongoing professional development and support for teachers in order to ensure the success of differentiated instruction in the classroom.

Overall, the purpose of this book is to provide educators with a comprehensive guide to implementing differentiated instruction in their classrooms, and to help them create a learning environment that meets the unique needs of all students, while promoting academic achievement and student success.

TABLE OF CONTENTS

ABOUT AUTHER

MR. MUJAHID BAKHT

LIFE HISTORY:- Mr. Bakht is a mature, experienced, extremely enthusiastic, energetic, administrator and thirty-six years have proven experience as a businessman in international marketing and public relations. Mr. Bakht is an International Real Estate Specialist, and Professional Business and Projects Consultant. He was born in Pakistan, Educated in Pakistan and USA. Presently American Citizen belongs to business-oriented family. Thirty-Seven years Resident of New York, USA.

BUSINESS HISTORY:- Mr. Bakht is a Founder & President of Atlas Amazon, LLC., Mr. Bakht is a business developer and multilingual business specialist in the Caribbean, South East Asia, and the Middle East emerging markets Mr. Bakht has served, met, and host many "Heads of the Countries" Also, maintain a close relationship with investors of high net worth in the USA.

CAREER:- Mr. Bakht has been engaged with many multinational companies in the field of international real estate investment, communication, technology, diamond, gold, mining, Pre-Feb housing, wind & solar energy, outsourcing management, and project consulting along with business partners & associates worldwide. Mr. Bakht has participated in major national and international conferences including participated in United Nations (U.N.O.) conferences.

TRAVEL:- Mr. Bakht is well-traveled and has visited many countries worldwide.

MANAGEMENT EXPERIENCE:- Thirty-Seven years of diversified experience in project consulting, marketing, and business management. As a Director of Marketing, Director of Public Relations, Director of International Affairs, Executive Vice President, President, CEO, and Chairman of many national & multinational companies, where he served previously. Mr. Bakht hired and trained many professionals as business consultants in international marketing and supervised them. Mr. Bakht is the author and publisher of multiple books.

CERTIFICATE OF ACHIEVEMENT; Achievement Award was presented to Mr. Bakht by Stephen Fossler for five years of continued growth and customer satisfaction from 1996 to 2001.

HONORS MEMBER; Madison Who's Who of Professionals, having demonstrated exemplary achievement and distinguished contributions to the business community, registered at the Library of Congress in Washington D.C. USA. (2007 & 2008)

HONORS MEMBER; Premiere Who's Who International, professional business executive having demonstrated exemplary achievement and distinguished contributions to the International business community, 2008 and 2009.

CERTIFICATES; Certificate of Authenticity from Bill Rodham Clinton, President of the United States, and Hillary Rodham Clinton First Lady, USA. (July 20, 2000);

CERTIFICATE OF AUTHENTICITY; from Terence R. McAuliffe, Chairman of Democratic National Committee, Tom Dachle, Senate Democratic Leader, Dick Gephardt, House Democratic Leader, USA. (June 16, 2001);

CERTIFICATE OF AUTHENTICITY; from Terence R. McAuliffe, Chairman of Democratic National Committee, USA. (April 16, 2002).

PERSONAL MEETINGS WITH DIGNITARIES:

Honorable. Teng-Hui-Lee, President of Taiwan. 1999.
Hon. Leonard Fernandez, President of the Dominican Republic. 1999.
Prince. Ahmed Fahad Al-Turki, (Saudi Arabia). 2000.
Benazir Bhutto, Prime Minister of Pakistan, 2001.
Dr. Keith Mitchell, Prime Minister of Grenada, West Indies. 2003-2004.
Pierre Charles, Prime Minister of Dominica, West Indies, 2003.
Mr. Charles Sovran, Foreign Minister of Dominica, 2003.
Robert H. O. Corbin Leader & Deputy-Prime-Minister (PNC) Guyana 2004.
Hon. P. J. Peterson, Prime Minister of Jamaica. 2004.
Dr. Kenny D. Anthony, Prime Minister of Saint Lucia, West Indies. 2005.

Hon. Owen Arthur, Prime Minister of Barbados, West Indies. 2005.

Michael de la Bastide, "Chief Justice" and President of the Caribbean Islands. 2005.

Mahmood M. Hussain, the Private Office of His Royal Highness. Dr. Sheikh-

Sultan Bin Khalifa Bin Zayed Al Nahyan, Abu-Dhabi, U.A.E. 2005.

Sultan S. Al Mansoori, Saeed & Mohammed Alnaboodah, Dubai, UAE 2005.

Ibrahim A. Gambari, Under-Secretary-General (United Nations) 2006.

Hon. Villasarao Deshmukh, Chief Minister of Maharashtra, India, 2006.

Hon. Ashok Chovan, Minister of Industries, Maharashtra, India, 2006.

Hon. Liu Bowie, Ambassador of China, United Nations, 2006.

Senator Einstein Louison, Ministry of Agriculture, Grenada.

Hon. Mark Isaac, Minister of State, Grenada, West Indies.

Hon. Brenda Hood, Minister for Tourism, Civil Aviation, Culture, Grenada.

Wayne Smith, Mayor, Township of Irvington, New Jersey, USA.

Orlando J. Moreno, Brigadier General & Military Advisor, (UNO) Venezuela.

As well as many more.

CHAPTER 1

INTRODUCTION

Differentiated instruction is an approach to teaching that involves adapting instruction to meet the needs of individual students. The aim of differentiated instruction is to create a learning environment that is responsive to the diversity of learners in the classroom, recognizing that each student has different learning needs, abilities, interests, and cultural backgrounds. Differentiated instruction recognizes that a "one size fits all" approach to teaching is ineffective, and that students require personalized instruction to achieve their full potential.

The concept of differentiated instruction has its roots in the work of Carol Ann Tomlinson, who first introduced the concept in the late 1990s. Tomlinson defines differentiated instruction as "an approach to teaching that advocates active planning for and attention to student differences in classrooms, in the context of high-quality curriculums" (Tomlinson, 2017, p. 3). In other words, differentiated instruction involves planning and delivering instruction that is tailored to the individual needs of students, while still ensuring that the curriculum is rigorous and meets the needs of all students.

One of the key principles of differentiated instruction is that instruction must be flexible and responsive to the needs of individual students. This involves adapting instruction in several ways, including content, process, product, and learning environment. Content refers to the material that is taught, while process refers to the methods and strategies used to teach the material. Product refers to the ways in which students demonstrate their learning, while learning environment refers to the physical and social context in which learning takes place.

Differentiated instruction involves a number of strategies for adapting instruction to meet the needs of individual students. These strategies include:

Flexible grouping: Grouping students according to their learning needs and abilities, and adjusting groups as needed to ensure that students are working with others who are at a similar level of understanding.

Tiered assignments: Assigning different tasks or activities to different groups of students based on their readiness level or interests.

Learning contracts: Working with individual students to develop personalized plans for learning, including goals, activities, and assessment.

Choice boards: Offering students a variety of options for demonstrating their learning, such as different types of projects or assessments.

Scaffolded instruction: Providing additional support to students who need it, such as extra practice, graphic organizers, or guided notes.

Varied assessments: Using a variety of assessment methods to evaluate student learning, such as performance tasks, projects, and portfolios.

Technology integration: Using technology to provide personalized instruction, such as adaptive software programs that adjust to the needs of individual students.

There are a number of benefits to using differentiated instruction in the classroom. One of the key benefits is that it allows teachers to meet the needs of individual students, which can lead to greater engagement and motivation. When students feel that their learning needs are being met, they are more likely to be interested in the material and more willing to participate in class. Differentiated instruction can also help to address the achievement gap, as it provides additional support and challenge to students who need it most.

Differentiated instruction also benefits teachers by providing a more flexible and responsive approach to instruction. Rather than teaching to the middle of the class, teachers are able to adapt instruction to meet the needs of all students, regardless of their ability level. This can lead to a more enjoyable and fulfilling teaching experience, as teachers are able to see the progress of individual students and adjust instruction accordingly.

Despite the benefits of differentiated instruction, there are also a number of challenges to implementing this approach. One of the biggest challenges is the amount of planning and preparation required. Differentiated instruction requires a significant amount of planning and preparation to ensure that instruction is tailored to the needs of individual students. This can be time-consuming and may require additional resources, such as materials and technology.

Another challenge is the need for teacher training and support. Teachers must be trained in the principles and strategies of differentiated instruction in order to effectively implement this approach in the classroom. This may require additional professional development opportunities, mentoring, or coaching.

Another challenge is the potential for equity issues to arise. Differentiated instruction can be challenging in terms of ensuring that all students have access to the same level of rigor and that no student is left behind. There is also the potential for students to be grouped in ways that reinforce stereotypes or bias, or for certain groups of students to be disproportionately represented in higher or lower ability groups.

To address these challenges, it is important for schools and districts to provide ongoing support and resources for teachers who are implementing differentiated instruction. This may include professional development opportunities, mentoring or coaching programs, and access to technology and other resources.

Differentiated instruction is an approach to teaching that involves adapting instruction to meet the needs of individual students. By recognizing the diversity of learners in the classroom and providing personalized instruction, differentiated instruction can lead to greater engagement and motivation among students, while also addressing the achievement gap. However, there are also challenges to implementing differentiated instruction, including the need for significant planning and preparation, teacher training and support, and the potential for equity issues to arise. With the right resources and support, however, differentiated instruction can be an effective approach to teaching that meets the needs of all students.

The importance of differentiating instruction for diverse learners

Differentiating instruction for diverse learners is a critical aspect of effective teaching. In today's diverse classrooms, students come from a variety of backgrounds, cultures, languages, and ability levels. Each student has unique learning needs and styles, and therefore, a one-size-fits-all approach to instruction is not effective. Differentiating instruction is the process of tailoring instruction to meet the individual needs of students, which is critical to ensure that all students have access to high-quality education that leads to academic and personal success. This essay will examine the importance of differentiating instruction for diverse learners, including the benefits and challenges of differentiated instruction, and strategies for effective implementation.

One of the primary benefits of differentiating instruction is that it allows teachers to meet the needs of all students, regardless of their background, culture, language, or ability level. Differentiated instruction recognizes that students have different learning needs, interests, and strengths, and therefore require different types and levels of support. By adapting instruction to meet the needs of individual students, teachers can create a learning environment that is responsive to the diversity of learners in the classroom. This can lead to greater engagement, motivation, and success among students.

Another benefit of differentiating instruction is that it can help to close the achievement gap. The achievement gap refers to the disparity in academic achievement between students from different backgrounds, cultures, and socio-economic levels. By providing personalized instruction that meets the needs of all students, teachers can help to address the root causes of the achievement gap, such as unequal access to resources, cultural bias, and implicit bias.

Differentiated instruction can also promote equity in the classroom. Equity means that all students have access to the same opportunities and resources, regardless of their background or ability level. By adapting instruction to meet the needs of individual students, teachers can ensure that all students have access to high-quality education that is tailored to their needs. This can help to address the achievement gap and promote social justice in the classroom.

Despite the benefits of differentiated instruction, there are also challenges to implementing this approach. One of the main challenges is the amount of planning and preparation required. Differentiated instruction requires teachers to develop multiple lessons and activities to meet the needs of individual students, which can be time-consuming and require significant planning and preparation. Teachers must also have a deep understanding of each student's learning needs, interests, and strengths, which can be challenging in a large classroom.

Another challenge is the need for teacher training and support. Teachers must be trained in the principles and strategies of differentiated instruction in order to effectively implement this approach in the classroom. This may require additional professional development opportunities, mentoring, or coaching. Teachers must also have access to technology and other resources that can support differentiated instruction.

To effectively implement differentiated instruction, teachers must use a variety of strategies and techniques. These strategies may include flexible grouping, tiered assignments, learning contracts, choice boards, scaffolded instruction, varied assessments, and technology integration. These strategies can help to ensure that all students are engaged and motivated, regardless of their background or ability level.

Flexible grouping is an effective strategy for differentiating instruction. This strategy involves grouping students according to their learning needs and abilities, and adjusting groups as needed to ensure that students are working with others who are at a similar level of understanding. This can help to ensure that students are challenged and engaged in their learning, while also providing additional support to students who need it.

Tiered assignments are another effective strategy for differentiating instruction. This strategy involves assigning different tasks or activities to different groups of students based on their readiness level or interests. This can help to ensure that students are working on tasks that are appropriate for their level of understanding, while also providing opportunities for students to pursue their interests.

Learning contracts are a personalized strategy for differentiating instruction. This strategy involves working with individual students to develop personalized plans for learning, including goals, activities, and assessment. This can help to ensure that students are engaged and motivated in their learning, as they have a direct say in what they will be learning and how they will be assessed.

Choice boards are another effective strategy for differentiating instruction. This strategy involves offering students a variety of options for demonstrating their learning, such as different types of projects or assessments. This can help to ensure that students are able to demonstrate their understanding in a way that is meaningful to them, while also providing additional opportunities for creativity and innovation.

Scaffolded instruction is an important strategy for differentiating instruction, particularly for students who require additional support. This strategy involves providing additional support to students who need it, such as extra practice, graphic organizers, or guided notes. This can help to ensure that all students are able to access the material and achieve success in their learning.

Varied assessments are also an important strategy for differentiating instruction. This strategy involves using a variety of assessment methods to evaluate student learning, such as performance tasks, projects, and portfolios. This can help to ensure that all students are able to demonstrate their understanding in a way that is meaningful to them, while also providing opportunities for creativity and innovation.

Technology integration is another important strategy for differentiating instruction. This strategy involves using technology to provide personalized instruction, such as adaptive software programs that adjust to the needs of individual students. This can help to ensure that all students are able to access the material and achieve success in their learning, regardless of their background or ability level.

Differentiating instruction for diverse learners is a critical aspect of effective teaching. By tailoring instruction to meet the individual needs of students, teachers can create a learning environment that is responsive to the diversity of learners in the classroom. This can lead to greater engagement, motivation, and success among students, and can help to close the achievement gap and promote equity in the classroom. Despite the challenges of implementing differentiated instruction, there are a variety of strategies and techniques that can be used to effectively differentiate instruction, including flexible grouping, tiered assignments, learning contracts, choice boards, scaffolded instruction, varied assessments, and technology integration. With the right training and support, teachers can effectively differentiate instruction to meet the needs of all students, regardless of their background or ability level.

The benefits of differentiated instruction

Differentiated instruction is an approach to teaching that tailors instruction to meet the individual needs of students. This approach recognizes that students have different learning styles, strengths, interests, and backgrounds, and therefore require different types and levels of support. Differentiated instruction offers a variety of benefits to both students and teachers. In this essay, we will examine the benefits of differentiated instruction.

One of the primary benefits of differentiated instruction is that it promotes student engagement and motivation. When students feel that instruction is tailored to their needs and interests, they are more likely to be engaged and motivated in their learning. Differentiated instruction allows students to work at their own pace and level, which can lead to a greater sense of autonomy and ownership over their learning. This can lead to a greater sense of enjoyment and satisfaction in the learning process, which can help to improve academic achievement.

Another benefit of differentiated instruction is that it improves academic achievement. When instruction is tailored to meet the individual needs of students, they are more likely to be successful in their learning. Differentiated instruction can help to address the achievement gap by providing additional support and challenge to students who need it most. By adapting instruction to meet the needs of all students, teachers can help to ensure that all students are able to access the curriculum and achieve success.

Differentiated instruction can also promote equity in the classroom. Equity means that all students have access to the same opportunities and resources, regardless of their background or ability level. By adapting instruction to meet the needs of individual students, teachers can ensure that all students have access to high-quality education that is tailored to their needs. This can help to address the achievement gap and promote social justice in the classroom.

Differentiated instruction can also improve teacher satisfaction and efficacy. When teachers are able to successfully differentiate instruction, they are more likely to feel a sense of accomplishment and satisfaction in their teaching. They are able to see the progress of individual students and adjust instruction accordingly, which can lead to a more enjoyable and fulfilling teaching experience. Differentiated instruction can also improve teacher efficacy by providing a more flexible and responsive approach to instruction. Rather than teaching to the middle of the class, teachers are able to adapt instruction to meet the needs of all students, regardless of their ability level.

Differentiated instruction can also promote critical thinking and problem-solving skills. When students are provided with opportunities to work at their own pace and level, they are more likely to be engaged in the learning process. They are able to ask questions, make connections, and think critically about the material. This can help to develop important critical thinking and problem-solving skills that are essential for success in school and beyond.

Differentiated instruction offers a variety of benefits to both students and teachers. By tailoring instruction to meet the individual needs of students, teachers can promote student engagement, improve academic achievement, promote equity, improve teacher satisfaction and efficacy, and promote critical thinking and problem-solving skills. Despite the challenges of implementing differentiated instruction, there are a variety of strategies and techniques that can be used to effectively differentiate instruction, including flexible grouping, tiered assignments, learning contracts, choice boards, scaffolded instruction, varied assessments, and technology integration. With the right training and support, teachers can effectively differentiate instruction to meet the needs of all students, regardless of their background or ability level.

The challenges of implementing differentiated instruction

Differentiated instruction is an approach to teaching that tailors instruction to meet the individual needs of students. This approach recognizes that students have different learning styles, strengths, interests, and backgrounds, and therefore require different types and levels of support. While differentiated instruction offers many benefits to both students and teachers, there are also several challenges associated with implementing this approach. In this essay, we will examine the challenges of implementing differentiated instruction, including planning and preparation, teacher training and support, equity issues, and assessment.

One of the primary challenges of implementing differentiated instruction is the amount of planning and preparation required. Differentiated instruction requires teachers to develop multiple lessons and activities to meet the needs of individual students, which can be time-consuming and require significant planning and preparation. Teachers must also have a deep understanding of each student's learning needs, interests, and strengths, which can be challenging in a large classroom. Teachers must also have access to resources such as materials and technology, to ensure that they can develop differentiated lessons and activities.

Another challenge of implementing differentiated instruction is the need for teacher training and support. Teachers must be trained in the principles and strategies of differentiated instruction in order to effectively implement this approach in the classroom. This may require additional professional development opportunities, mentoring, or coaching. Teachers must also have access to resources such as technology and other instructional materials that can support differentiated instruction. In addition, teachers need ongoing support and feedback to ensure that they are effectively implementing differentiated instruction in the classroom.

Another challenge of implementing differentiated instruction is the potential for equity issues to arise. Differentiated instruction can be challenging in terms of ensuring that all students have access to the same level of rigor and that no student is left behind. There is also the potential for students to be grouped in ways that reinforce stereotypes or bias, or for certain groups of students to be disproportionately represented in higher or lower ability groups. Teachers must be mindful of these potential equity issues and take steps to ensure that all students have access to high-quality instruction and that no student is disadvantaged by the approach.

Assessment is also a challenge associated with implementing differentiated instruction. Differentiated instruction involves using a variety of assessments to evaluate student learning, such as performance tasks, projects, and portfolios. This can be challenging for teachers who are used to using traditional forms of assessment such as tests and quizzes. Teachers must be able to develop and use a variety of assessments to effectively evaluate student learning and provide feedback to students. In addition, teachers must be able to use assessment data to adjust instruction and ensure that students are making progress.

Another challenge of implementing differentiated instruction is managing the different needs of students. Differentiated instruction requires teachers to provide different levels of support and challenge to different students. This can be challenging to manage in a large classroom. Teachers must be able to effectively manage classroom behavior and ensure that all students are engaged in the learning process. They must also be able to provide appropriate levels of support and challenge to individual students, without neglecting the needs of other students.

To address these challenges, it is important for schools and districts to provide ongoing support and resources for teachers who are implementing differentiated instruction. This may include professional development opportunities, mentoring or coaching programs, and access to technology and other resources. Schools and districts must also be committed to ensuring that all students have access to high-quality instruction, regardless of their background or ability level. They must be willing to address equity issues and provide support to teachers to effectively implement differentiated instruction in the classroom.

Differentiated instruction is an approach to teaching that tailors instruction to meet the individual needs of students. While differentiated instruction offers many benefits, including promoting student engagement, improving academic achievement, promoting equity, and promoting critical thinking and problem-solving skills, there are also several challenges associated with implementing this approach. These challenges include planning and preparation, teacher training and support, equity issues

CHAPTER 2

UNDERSTANDING DIVERSITY IN THE CLASSROOM

Diversity is a term used to describe the differences that exist among individuals in terms of their race, ethnicity, culture, language, religion, gender, sexual orientation, socio-economic status, and ability, among others. In the context of the classroom, diversity can take many forms, each of which has its unique characteristics, opportunities, and challenges. In this essay, we will explore the different types of diversity that exist in the classroom, their significance, and ways to manage them.

Racial and Ethnic Diversity

One of the most noticeable types of diversity in the classroom is racial and ethnic diversity. This refers to the differences that exist among students based on their race, ethnicity, and cultural background. The impact of racial and ethnic diversity is that it leads to a rich exchange of ideas, perspectives, and experiences. However, it can also lead to challenges such as cultural misunderstandings and stereotypes. Teachers can address these challenges by promoting cultural sensitivity and inclusivity, using diverse teaching materials, and creating opportunities for students to share their cultural experiences.

Linguistic Diversity

Linguistic diversity refers to the differences that exist among students based on their language backgrounds. This can include students who speak different languages at home or who have different levels of proficiency in the language of instruction. The impact of linguistic diversity is that it can lead to linguistic and cultural enrichment, as well as communication challenges. Teachers can address these challenges by using a variety of instructional strategies, such as visual aids and hands-on activities, to support students' comprehension. Teachers can also create opportunities for students to share their language and cultural experiences.

Gender Diversity

Gender diversity refers to the differences that exist among students based on their gender identity and expression. This can include students who identify as male, female, non-binary, or transgender. The impact of gender diversity is that it can lead to a richer understanding of gender issues, as well as challenges related to stereotypes and discrimination. Teachers can address these challenges by promoting gender inclusivity, using gender-neutral language, and providing opportunities for students to explore their gender identity and expression.

Socioeconomic Diversity

Socioeconomic diversity refers to the differences that exist among students based on their family income, education level, and occupation. The impact of socioeconomic diversity is that it can lead to a better understanding of the challenges faced by students from disadvantaged backgrounds, as well as challenges related to privilege and classism. Teachers can address these challenges by promoting equity and inclusion, providing resources and support for students from disadvantaged backgrounds, and creating opportunities for students to learn about and appreciate different socioeconomic backgrounds.

Religious Diversity

Religious diversity refers to the differences that exist among students based on their religious beliefs and practices. This can include students who follow different religions or who have no religious affiliation. The impact of religious diversity is that it can lead to a richer understanding of different religious traditions and practices, as well as challenges related to religious stereotypes and discrimination. Teachers can address these challenges by promoting religious tolerance and inclusivity, using diverse teaching materials that reflect different religious traditions, and creating opportunities for students to learn about and appreciate different religious beliefs and practices.

Ability Diversity

Ability diversity refers to the differences that exist among students based on their physical, sensory, intellectual, or emotional abilities. This can include students with disabilities or students with different learning styles. The impact of ability diversity is that it can lead to a better understanding of the challenges faced by students with disabilities or different learning styles, as well as challenges related to ableism and discrimination. Teachers can address these challenges by promoting accessibility and inclusivity, providing accommodations and support for students with disabilities, and using diverse teaching strategies that support different learning styles.

Cultural Diversity

Cultural diversity refers to the differences that exist among students based on their cultural practices, beliefs, and values. Cultural diversity is closely related to racial and ethnic diversity but focuses more on the differences that exist among students based on their cultural practices, beliefs, and values. This can include students from different countries or regions with different cultural traditions and customs. The impact of cultural diversity is that it can lead to a richer understanding of different cultural traditions and practices, as well as challenges related to cultural misunderstandings and stereotypes. Teachers can address these challenges by promoting cultural sensitivity and inclusivity, using diverse teaching materials that reflect different cultural traditions, and creating opportunities for students to learn about and appreciate different cultural practices.

Generational Diversity

Generational diversity refers to the differences that exist among students based on their age and generation. This can include students from different generations such as Baby Boomers, Generation X, Millennials, and Generation Z. The impact of generational diversity is that it can lead to a richer understanding of different generational perspectives and values, as well as challenges related to generational stereotypes and misunderstandings. Teachers can address these challenges by promoting generational inclusivity, using teaching materials that reflect different generational perspectives, and creating opportunities for students to learn about and appreciate different generational values and experiences.

Geographic Diversity

Geographic diversity refers to the differences that exist among students based on their geographic location. This can include students from different parts of the country or different countries altogether. The impact of geographic diversity is that it can lead to a richer understanding of different geographic regions and cultures, as well as challenges related to geographic stereotypes and misunderstandings. Teachers can address these challenges by promoting geographic inclusivity, using teaching materials that reflect different geographic regions and cultures, and creating opportunities for students to learn about and appreciate different geographic locations and experiences.

Cognitive Diversity

Cognitive diversity refers to the differences that exist among students based on their cognitive abilities and thinking styles. This can include students with different cognitive abilities such as creativity, critical thinking, and problem-solving skills. The impact of cognitive diversity is that it can lead to a richer understanding of different thinking styles and approaches, as well as challenges related to cognitive stereotypes and misunderstandings. Teachers can address these challenges by promoting cognitive inclusivity, using teaching materials that reflect different thinking styles and approaches, and creating opportunities for students to learn about and appreciate different cognitive abilities.

Diversity in the classroom takes many forms, each with its unique characteristics, opportunities, and challenges. Teachers can manage these diverse classrooms by promoting inclusivity, using diverse teaching materials, providing accommodations and support for students with disabilities or different learning styles, and creating opportunities for students to learn about and appreciate different cultures, traditions, values, and experiences. By doing so, teachers can create a more equitable and inclusive learning environment that celebrates and values the diversity of all students.

The impact of diversity on learning

Diversity in the classroom can have a significant impact on learning for both students and teachers. A diverse classroom is one that includes individuals from different cultural, ethnic, racial, linguistic, religious, socioeconomic, and ability backgrounds. The following essay will explore the impact of diversity on learning and how it can benefit students and teachers.

Improved Critical Thinking and Problem Solving

One of the significant benefits of diversity in the classroom is that it can lead to improved critical thinking and problem solving. When students are exposed to different perspectives and ways of thinking, it can challenge their assumptions and encourage them to think critically. This can lead to a more comprehensive understanding of the subject matter and help students develop problem-solving skills that are necessary in the real world.

Increased Creativity and Innovation

Diversity can also lead to increased creativity and innovation. When students from different backgrounds collaborate, they bring unique experiences, ideas, and perspectives to the table. This can lead to new and innovative solutions to problems and help students develop a more creative approach to learning.

Enhanced Cultural Competence and Empathy

Another benefit of diversity in the classroom is that it can enhance cultural competence and empathy. When students are exposed to different cultures and ways of life, they can develop a greater understanding and appreciation for diversity. This can help them develop empathy and respect for people who are different from themselves, which is an essential skill in today's globalized world.

Improved Communication Skills

Diversity can also lead to improved communication skills. When students are exposed to different languages and communication styles, they can learn how to communicate effectively with people from different backgrounds. This can lead to better teamwork and collaboration, as well as improved interpersonal skills that are necessary in the real world.

Increased Academic Achievement

Research has shown that diversity in the classroom can lead to increased academic achievem1ent. When students are exposed to different perspectives and ways of thinking, it can lead to a more comprehensive understanding of the subject matter. This can help students perform better on exams and assignments, as well as develop a more profound understanding of the subject matter.

Improved Self-Esteem and Confidence

Diversity can also lead to improved self-esteem and confidence. When students feel included and valued in the classroom, it can boost their self-esteem and confidence. This can lead to improved academic performance, as well as better mental health and wellbeing.

Better Preparation for the Real World

Finally, diversity in the classroom can better prepare students for the real world. In today's globalized world, students need to be able to work effectively with people from different backgrounds. Exposure to diversity in the classroom can help students develop the skills and attitudes necessary to succeed in today's diverse workforce.

Overall, diversity in the classroom can have a significant impact on learning. It can lead to improved critical thinking and problem solving, increased creativity and innovation, enhanced cultural competence and empathy, improved communication skills, increased academic achievement, improved self-esteem and confidence, and better preparation for the real world. Teachers can promote diversity in the classroom by using diverse teaching materials, creating opportunities for students to share their experiences and perspectives, and promoting inclusivity and respect for diversity.

The importance of cultural responsiveness in teaching

Cultural responsiveness in teaching is the ability to understand, respect, and appreciate the cultural backgrounds and experiences of students. It involves creating a safe and inclusive learning environment where all students feel valued and supported, regardless of their cultural, linguistic, or socioeconomic background. In this essay, we will discuss the importance of cultural responsiveness in teaching and how it can benefit both students and teachers.

Promotes Equity and Inclusion

Cultural responsiveness in teaching is essential for promoting equity and inclusion in the classroom. It acknowledges the unique cultural backgrounds and experiences of each student and recognizes the impact that these factors can have on learning. By creating an inclusive learning environment, cultural responsiveness can ensure that all students have equal opportunities to succeed academically and personally.

Increases Student Engagement

Cultural responsiveness can also increase student engagement in the classroom. When students feel that their cultural backgrounds and experiences are valued and respected, they are more likely to be motivated to participate in class and to engage with the subject matter. This can lead to improved academic performance and a more positive learning experience.

Improves Teacher-Student Relationships

Cultural responsiveness can also improve teacher-student relationships. When teachers take the time to understand and appreciate the cultural backgrounds and experiences of their students, they can build trust and rapport with them. This can lead to a more positive and supportive learning environment and can help students feel more comfortable asking questions and seeking help.

Enhances Critical Thinking and Problem-Solving Skills

Cultural responsiveness can also enhance critical thinking and problem-solving skills. By exposing students to diverse perspectives and experiences, it can challenge their assumptions and encourage them to think critically. This can lead to a more comprehensive understanding of the subject matter and can help students develop problem-solving skills that are necessary in the real world.

Promotes Cultural Competence

Cultural responsiveness can also promote cultural competence, which is the ability to understand and appreciate the cultural differences and similarities between people. By promoting cultural competence in the classroom, teachers can prepare students for the diverse world they will encounter outside of school. This can help students develop empathy and respect for people who are different from themselves and can lead to better interpersonal relationships in their personal and professional lives.

Improves Academic Performance

Research has shown that cultural responsiveness can improve academic performance. When teachers use culturally responsive teaching practices, they can better engage and motivate students, leading to improved academic outcomes. This is especially true for students from underrepresented backgrounds, who may have experienced cultural mismatch in traditional classroom settings.

Fosters a Sense of Community

Finally, cultural responsiveness in teaching can foster a sense of community in the classroom. When students feel that their cultural backgrounds and experiences are valued and respected, they are more likely to feel connected to their classmates and to the school community as a whole. This can lead to a more positive and supportive learning environment and can improve overall student wellbeing.

Cultural responsiveness in teaching is essential for creating a safe and inclusive learning environment where all students feel valued and supported. It promotes equity and inclusion, increases student engagement, improves teacher-student relationships, enhances critical thinking and problem-solving skills, promotes cultural competence, improves academic performance, and fosters a sense of community. Teachers can promote cultural responsiveness by using culturally responsive teaching practices, creating opportunities for students to share their experiences and perspectives, and promoting inclusivity and respect for diversity in the classroom.

Addressing cultural stereotypes and biases

Cultural stereotypes and biases can have a significant impact on how individuals perceive and interact with people from different cultural backgrounds. These biases can affect our attitudes, beliefs, and behaviors, and can contribute to discrimination and inequality. In this essay, we will discuss the importance of addressing cultural stereotypes and biases and provide strategies for promoting cultural understanding and inclusivity.

Educate Yourself

The first step in addressing cultural stereotypes and biases is to educate yourself about different cultures and their histories. This can help you to better understand and appreciate cultural differences and similarities, and can help you to challenge your own assumptions and biases. You can educate yourself by reading books, watching documentaries, attending cultural events, and talking to people from different cultural backgrounds.

Examine Your Own Biases

It is important to examine your own biases and assumptions about different cultures. Reflect on your own experiences and how they may have shaped your beliefs and attitudes towards certain cultural groups. You can also take implicit bias tests to identify any unconscious biases you may have. Once you are aware of your biases, you can take steps to challenge and overcome them.

Promote Cultural Understanding and Inclusivity

Promoting cultural understanding and inclusivity is essential for addressing cultural stereotypes and biases. This can be achieved by creating opportunities for people from different cultural backgrounds to share their experiences and perspectives. This can include hosting cultural events, inviting guest speakers from different cultural backgrounds, and incorporating diverse perspectives into curricula and discussions.

Challenge Stereotypes and Biases

It is important to challenge stereotypes and biases when you encounter them. This can involve speaking up when you hear someone make a derogatory comment about a particular cultural group, or correcting misinformation about a particular culture. By challenging stereotypes and biases, you can help to promote cultural understanding and inclusivity.

Be Open-Minded

Being open-minded is essential for addressing cultural stereotypes and biases. It is important to approach different cultures with an open and curious mindset, rather than with preconceived ideas and assumptions. This can help you to better understand and appreciate cultural differences and similarities, and can promote cultural understanding and inclusivity.

Model Inclusive Behavior

Modeling inclusive behavior is essential for promoting cultural understanding and inclusivity. This can involve treating people from different cultural backgrounds with respect and empathy, actively listening to their perspectives, and valuing their contributions. By modeling inclusive behavior, you can help to create a safe and inclusive environment for people from different cultural backgrounds.

Practice Empathy

Practicing empathy is essential for addressing cultural stereotypes and biases. This involves putting yourself in someone else's shoes and trying to understand their experiences and perspectives. By practicing empathy, you can better understand and appreciate the challenges and experiences of people from different cultural backgrounds, and can promote cultural understanding and inclusivity.

Addressing cultural stereotypes and biases is essential for promoting cultural understanding and inclusivity. Educating yourself, examining your own biases, promoting cultural understanding and inclusivity, challenging stereotypes and biases, being open-minded, modeling inclusive behavior, and practicing empathy are all strategies that can help to address cultural stereotypes and biases. By working to address cultural stereotypes and biases, we can promote a more inclusive and equitable society where everyone feels valued and respected.

CHAPTER 3

DIFFERENTIATED INSTRUCTION IN PRACTICE

Differentiated instruction is a teaching approach that recognizes the unique learning needs of each student and provides individualized instruction to support their academic growth. The principles of differentiated instruction involve identifying and addressing students' diverse learning needs, providing a variety of instructional strategies, and assessing student progress to adjust instruction accordingly. In this essay, we will discuss the principles of differentiated instruction and strategies for implementing it effectively in the classroom.

Understanding Students' Diverse Learning Needs

The first principle of differentiated instruction is to understand the diverse learning needs of each student. This involves recognizing that students come to the classroom with a range of abilities, interests, and learning styles. To effectively differentiate instruction, teachers must assess each student's strengths and weaknesses, identify their learning style, and take into account their cultural and linguistic background.

Providing a Variety of Instructional Strategies

The second principle of differentiated instruction is to provide a variety of instructional strategies to meet the diverse learning needs of students. This involves using different teaching methods such as visual, auditory, and kinesthetic activities, as well as offering students a variety of materials to support their learning. Differentiated instruction also involves providing opportunities for student choice in learning tasks and assignments.

Adjusting Instruction Based on Assessment Data

The third principle of differentiated instruction is to adjust instruction based on ongoing assessment data. This involves monitoring student progress and adjusting instruction accordingly. Teachers must use a variety of assessment methods such as formative and summative assessments, observation, and student feedback to gather data about student learning. Based on this data, teachers can adjust their instruction to better meet the needs of their students.

Fostering a Positive Learning Environment

The fourth principle of differentiated instruction is to foster a positive learning environment that supports student learning. This involves creating a classroom culture that values diversity and encourages collaboration and mutual respect. Teachers must also provide opportunities for student-centered learning, such as project-based learning and cooperative learning, that support student engagement and motivation.

Strategies for Implementing Differentiated Instruction

Flexible Grouping

Flexible grouping is a key strategy for implementing differentiated instruction. This involves grouping students based on their academic needs and providing instruction that meets their individual needs. Teachers can use different grouping strategies such as whole-class instruction, small-group instruction, and individual instruction to meet the diverse needs of their students.

Varied Instructional Strategies

Providing varied instructional strategies is another effective strategy for implementing differentiated instruction. Teachers can use a range of teaching methods such as lecture, discussion, hands-on activities, and multimedia resources to meet the diverse learning needs of their students. Teachers can also provide students with multiple ways to demonstrate their understanding such as written assignments, projects, and presentations.

Scaffolded Instruction

Scaffolded instruction is another effective strategy for implementing differentiated instruction. This involves breaking down complex tasks into smaller, manageable steps and providing students with support as they work through the task. Teachers can provide scaffolding through modeling, prompts, and visual aids to help students achieve success.

Student Choice

Providing student choice is a powerful strategy for promoting student engagement and motivation in differentiated instruction. This involves giving students opportunities to choose their own learning tasks and assignments based on their interests and abilities. Teachers can provide a range of options such as reading assignments, writing prompts, and creative projects to support student choice.

Ongoing Assessment

Ongoing assessment is a critical strategy for implementing differentiated instruction. Teachers must use a variety of assessment methods such as formative and summative assessments, observation, and student feedback to gather data about student learning. Based on this data, teachers can adjust their instruction to better meet the needs of their students.

Strategies for differentiating instruction

Differentiated instruction is a teaching approach that recognizes the unique learning needs of each student and provides individualized instruction to support their academic growth. To effectively differentiate instruction, teachers must assess each student's strengths and weaknesses, identify their learning style, and take into account their cultural and linguistic background. In this essay, we will discuss strategies for differentiating instruction in the classroom.

Use of Technology

One effective strategy for differentiating instruction is the use of technology. Technology can provide students with access to a range of instructional materials that support their learning. For example, teachers can use interactive whiteboards, educational apps, and online resources to provide students with engaging and interactive learning experiences. Additionally, technology can provide opportunities for students to work at their own pace and receive immediate feedback on their progress.

Flexible Grouping

Flexible grouping is another effective strategy for differentiating instruction. This involves grouping students based on their academic needs and providing instruction that meets their individual needs. Teachers can use different grouping strategies such as whole-class instruction, small-group instruction, and individual instruction to meet the diverse needs of their students. Additionally, flexible grouping can provide opportunities for peer collaboration and support.

Varied Instructional Strategies

Providing varied instructional strategies is another effective strategy for differentiating instruction. Teachers can use a range of teaching methods such as lecture, discussion, hands-on activities, and multimedia resources to meet the diverse learning needs of their students. Teachers can also provide students with multiple ways to demonstrate their understanding such as written assignments, projects, and presentations.

Scaffolded Instruction

Scaffolded instruction is another effective strategy for differentiating instruction. This involves breaking down complex tasks into smaller, manageable steps and providing students with support as they work through the task. Teachers can provide scaffolding through modeling, prompts, and visual aids to help students achieve success. Additionally, scaffolding can provide opportunities for students to work at their own pace and receive targeted support.

Student Choice

Providing student choice is a powerful strategy for promoting student engagement and motivation in differentiated instruction. This involves giving students opportunities to choose their own learning tasks and assignments based on their interests and abilities. Teachers can provide a range of options such as reading assignments, writing prompts, and creative projects to support student choice. Additionally, student choice can provide opportunities for student-led learning and self-directed learning.

Differentiated Assessments

Differentiated assessments are another effective strategy for differentiating instruction. This involves using a range of assessment methods that align with the diverse learning needs of students. Teachers can use formative and summative assessments, observation, and student feedback to gather data about student learning. Additionally, teachers can provide different assessment options such as oral presentations, written assignments, and projects to support student success.

Differentiated Content

Differentiated content is another effective strategy for differentiating instruction. This involves providing students with different levels of content that align with their academic needs. Teachers can use a range of materials such as textbooks, articles, and online resources to provide students with differentiated content. Additionally, teachers can provide additional resources and support for students who require additional assistance with the content.

Differentiated Process

Differentiated process is another effective strategy for differentiating instruction. This involves providing students with different ways to engage with the content and learn the material. Teachers can provide different processes such as hands-on activities, independent study, and collaborative projects to support student learning. Additionally, teachers can provide additional support and resources for students who require additional assistance with the process.

Adapting instruction to individual student needs

Adapting instruction to individual student needs is a key component of effective teaching. Every student is unique and has their own learning needs, strengths, and challenges. Therefore, teachers must be able to adapt their instruction to meet the diverse needs of their students. In this essay, we will discuss strategies for adapting instruction to individual student needs.

Assessing Individual Needs

The first step in adapting instruction to individual student needs is to assess each student's strengths, weaknesses, learning styles, and interests. Teachers can use a range of assessment methods such as observation, informal assessments, formal assessments, and student feedback to gather data about student learning. This information can help teachers to identify individual student needs and design instruction that meets those needs.

Differentiated Instruction

Differentiated instruction is an effective strategy for adapting instruction to individual student needs. This approach involves providing instruction that is tailored to meet the diverse needs of students. Teachers can use a range of instructional strategies such as flexible grouping, varied instructional strategies, scaffolded instruction, student choice, and differentiated assessments to meet the diverse needs of their students. Additionally, differentiated instruction can provide opportunities for students to work at their own pace and receive targeted support.

Personalized Learning

Personalized learning is another effective strategy for adapting instruction to individual student needs. This approach involves tailoring instruction to meet the unique needs and interests of each student. Teachers can use a range of instructional methods such as project-based learning, inquiry-based learning, and experiential learning to support personalized learning. Additionally, personalized learning can provide opportunities for student-led learning and self-directed learning.

Student-Centered Instruction

Student-centered instruction is another effective strategy for adapting instruction to individual student needs. This approach involves placing the student at the center of the learning process and tailoring instruction to meet their individual needs. Teachers can use a range of instructional methods such as inquiry-based learning, collaborative learning, and experiential learning to support student-centered instruction. Additionally, student-centered instruction can provide opportunities for peer collaboration and support.

Universal Design for Learning

Universal Design for Learning (UDL) is another effective strategy for adapting instruction to individual student needs. UDL is an approach to teaching that provides multiple ways of accessing information and demonstrating understanding. Teachers can use a range of materials and resources such as audio, video, text, and interactive media to support UDL. Additionally, UDL can provide opportunities for students to engage with the content in ways that are meaningful and relevant to them.

Response to Intervention

Response to Intervention (RTI) is another effective strategy for adapting instruction to individual student needs. RTI is a framework that provides targeted support and intervention to students who are struggling academically or behaviorally. Teachers can use a range of assessment methods to identify students who require additional support and provide targeted interventions that meet their individual needs. Additionally, RTI can provide opportunities for early intervention and support to prevent academic and behavioral difficulties from becoming more severe.

Data-Driven Instruction

Data-driven instruction is another effective strategy for adapting instruction to individual student needs. This approach involves using data to inform instruction and make decisions about how to best support student learning. Teachers can use a range of assessment methods such as formative and summative assessments, student work samples, and observation to gather data about student learning. This data can be used to design instruction that meets the diverse needs of students and provides targeted support.

Adapting instruction to individual student needs is a key component of effective teaching. Strategies for adapting instruction to individual student needs include assessing individual needs, differentiated instruction, personalized learning, student-centered instruction, Universal Design for Learning, response to intervention, and data-driven instruction. By adapting instruction to meet the diverse needs of their students, teachers can better support their academic growth and success.

Differentiating instruction for mixed-ability groups

In any classroom, there are students who have different abilities, skills, interests, and learning styles. Differentiating instruction for mixed-ability groups is an essential strategy for ensuring that every student has the opportunity to learn and grow. Differentiating instruction refers to providing different levels of support and challenge to students based on their individual needs. In this essay, we will discuss strategies for differentiating instruction for mixed-ability groups.

Assessing Student Needs

The first step in differentiating instruction for mixed-ability groups is to assess each student's strengths, weaknesses, learning styles, and interests. Teachers can use a range of assessment methods such as observation, informal assessments, formal assessments, and student feedback to gather data about student learning. This information can help teachers to identify individual student needs and design instruction that meets those needs.

Flexible Grouping

Flexible grouping is an effective strategy for differentiating instruction for mixed-ability groups. This approach involves grouping students based on their individual needs and abilities. Teachers can use a range of grouping methods such as whole-class instruction, small-group instruction, pairs, and individual instruction to meet the diverse needs of their students. Additionally, flexible grouping can provide opportunities for students to work with peers who have similar abilities or different abilities, allowing them to learn from each other.

Varied Instructional Strategies

Varied instructional strategies are another effective strategy for differentiating instruction for mixed-ability groups. This approach involves using a range of instructional methods such as direct instruction, inquiry-based learning, project-based learning, and problem-based learning to support student learning. Teachers can use different instructional strategies to provide different levels of support and challenge to students based on their individual needs.

Scaffolded Instruction

Scaffolded instruction is another effective strategy for differentiating instruction for mixed-ability groups. This approach involves providing different levels of support and challenge to students based on their individual needs. Teachers can use a range of instructional strategies such as modeling, guided practice, and independent practice to provide scaffolded instruction to their students. Additionally, scaffolded instruction can provide opportunities for students to work at their own pace and receive targeted support.

Student Choice

Student choice is another effective strategy for differentiating instruction for mixed-ability groups. This approach involves providing students with choices about how they learn, what they learn, and how they demonstrate their understanding. Teachers can use a range of instructional methods such as choice boards, menus, and contract-based learning to support student choice. Additionally, student choice can provide opportunities for students to engage with the content in ways that are meaningful and relevant to them.

Differentiated Assessments

Differentiated assessments are another effective strategy for differentiating instruction for mixed-ability groups. This approach involves providing different levels of assessment to students based on their individual needs. Teachers can use a range of assessment methods such as performance assessments, alternative assessments, and formative assessments to support differentiated assessments. Additionally, differentiated assessments can provide opportunities for students to demonstrate their understanding in ways that are meaningful and relevant to them.

Individualized Instruction

Individualized instruction is another effective strategy for differentiating instruction for mixed-ability groups. This approach involves providing instruction that is tailored to meet the unique needs and interests of each student. Teachers can use a range of instructional methods such as personalized learning plans, independent study, and mentorship to support individualized instruction. Additionally, individualized instruction can provide opportunities for students to work at their own pace and receive targeted support.

Collaborative Learning

Collaborative learning is another effective strategy for differentiating instruction for mixed-ability groups. This approach involves working in groups to achieve a common goal. Teachers can use a range of instructional methods such as group projects, group discussions, and cooperative learning to support collaborative learning. Additionally, collaborative learning can provide opportunities for students.

Technology Integration

Technology integration is another effective strategy for differentiating instruction for mixed-ability groups. This approach involves using technology to provide personalized and interactive learning experiences for students. Teachers can use a range of technology tools such as educational apps, interactive whiteboards, and online learning platforms to support technology integration. Additionally, technology integration can provide opportunities for students to engage with the content in ways that are meaningful and relevant to them.

Ongoing Assessment and Feedback

Ongoing assessment and feedback are critical strategies for differentiating instruction for mixed-ability groups. This approach involves regularly assessing student progress and providing targeted feedback to support student learning. Teachers can use a range of assessment methods such as formative assessments, self-assessments, and peer assessments to support ongoing assessment and feedback. Additionally, ongoing assessment and feedback can provide opportunities for students to monitor their own progress and take ownership of their learning.

Teacher Collaboration

Teacher collaboration is another effective strategy for differentiating instruction for mixed-ability groups. This approach involves working with other teachers, specialists, and support staff to design and implement instructional strategies that meet the diverse needs of students. Teachers can use a range of collaborative methods such as co-teaching, team teaching, and professional learning communities to support teacher collaboration. Additionally, teacher collaboration can provide opportunities for teachers to share resources, expertise, and best practices.

Parent and Community Involvement

Parent and community involvement are critical strategies for differentiating instruction for mixed-ability groups. This approach involves engaging families and community members in the educational process and leveraging their support to enhance student learning. Teachers can use a range of involvement methods such as parent-teacher conferences, family nights, and community partnerships to support parent and community involvement. Additionally, parent and community involvement can provide opportunities for students to learn from diverse perspectives and experiences.

Differentiating instruction for mixed-ability groups is essential for ensuring that every student has the opportunity to learn and grow. Teachers can use a range of strategies such as flexible grouping, varied instructional strategies, scaffolded instruction, student choice, differentiated assessments, individualized instruction, collaborative learning, technology integration, ongoing assessment and feedback, teacher collaboration, and parent and community involvement to meet the diverse needs of their students. By implementing these strategies, teachers can create a learning environment that supports student learning, engagement, and success.

CHAPTER 4

ASSESSING STUDENT NEEDS

S tudents learn in different ways and have unique learning preferences. Understanding student learning styles can help teachers create instructional strategies that engage and support students in the learning process. This paper will explore the different learning styles, including visual, auditory, kinesthetic, and tactile learning styles, and provide strategies for accommodating each learning style in the classroom.

Visual Learning Style

Visual learners prefer to learn by seeing and observing information. They often learn best through visual aids such as pictures, diagrams, and charts. Visual learners tend to be good at spatial reasoning, remembering visual details, and creating mental images.

Accommodating Visual Learners

Use Visual Aids: Teachers can incorporate visual aids such as pictures, diagrams, and charts to support visual learners.

Graphic Organizers: Graphic organizers such as mind maps, Venn diagrams, and flowcharts can help visual learners organize information and make connections between concepts.

Whiteboard: Using a whiteboard can help visual learners follow along and see the organization of the lesson.

Videos: Videos can help visual learners understand concepts by providing visual examples.

Highlighting and Underlining: Highlighting and underlining important information in texts can help visual learners focus on key concepts.

Auditory Learning Style

Auditory learners prefer to learn by listening and speaking. They tend to process information best through sounds and verbal instructions. They are good at remembering information they have heard and can easily follow spoken directions.

Accommodating Auditory Learners

Lectures: Teachers can use lectures to help auditory learners learn and process information.

Discussion Groups: Discussion groups can allow auditory learners to actively participate and engage with the content.

Audio Recordings: Providing audio recordings of lessons can help auditory learners reinforce learning and review material.

Verbal Explanations: Teachers can explain concepts verbally to support auditory learners.

Mnemonics: Mnemonics such as acronyms and rhymes can help auditory learners remember information.

Kinesthetic Learning Style

Kinesthetic learners prefer to learn by doing and actively participating in the learning process. They tend to process information best through physical movement and tactile experiences. They are good at remembering information through physical memory and tend to be hands-on learners.

Accommodating Kinesthetic Learners

Hands-On Activities: Teachers can incorporate hands-on activities such as experiments and simulations to support kinesthetic learners.

Movement Breaks: Allowing students to take movement breaks can help kinesthetic learners stay focused and engaged.

Manipulatives: Manipulatives such as blocks and puzzles can help kinesthetic learners understand concepts through physical touch.

Role-Playing: Role-playing activities can help kinesthetic learners engage in the content and make connections to real-life scenarios.

Field Trips: Field trips can provide kinesthetic learners with hands-on experiences that relate to the content being taught.

Tactile Learning Style

Tactile learners prefer to learn through touch and physical contact with objects. They tend to process information best through hands-on experiences and need to be physically engaged in the learning process. They are good at remembering information through physical memory and tend to be hands-on learners.

Accommodating Tactile Learners

Hands-On Activities: Teachers can incorporate hands-on activities such as building and making to support tactile learners.

Manipulatives: Manipulatives such as blocks and puzzles can help tactile learners understand concepts through physical touch.

Movement Breaks: Allowing students to take movement breaks can help tactile learners stay focused and engaged.

Touching Textures: Allowing tactile learners to touch different textures such as sand or fabric can help them engage with the content.

Field Trips: Field trips can provide tactile learners with hands-on experiences that relate to Accommodating Multiple Learning Styles

It is important for teachers to understand that students may not fit into just one learning style category, and that they may have a combination of preferences. Therefore, it is important to incorporate multiple strategies to accommodate different learning styles. Here are some strategies for accommodating multiple learning styles:

Multi-Modal Presentations: Incorporating a variety of visual aids, auditory explanations, and hands-on activities can help engage students with different learning styles.

Choice Boards: Providing students with a choice of activities can allow them to choose activities that cater to their preferred learning style.

Differentiated Learning Centers: Creating learning centers that focus on different learning styles can help students engage with the content in different ways.

Flexible Seating: Allowing students to choose their seating arrangements can help accommodate different learning preferences.

Student Reflection: Encouraging students to reflect on their own learning preferences can help them understand their own learning styles and advocate for themselves.

Understanding student learning styles can help teachers create instructional strategies that support and engage students in the learning process. Teachers can accommodate different learning styles by incorporating visual aids, auditory explanations, hands-on activities, and tactile experiences. Additionally, teachers can accommodate multiple learning styles by providing multi-modal presentations, choice boards, differentiated learning centers, flexible seating, and encouraging student reflection. By incorporating strategies that support different learning styles, teachers can create a more inclusive and engaging learning environment that caters to the diverse needs of their students.

Using formative and summative assessments to guide instruction

Assessment is a critical component of the teaching and learning process. Formative and summative assessments are two types of assessments that teachers use to guide instruction and measure student progress. Formative assessments are used to monitor student learning throughout the instructional process, while summative assessments are used to evaluate student learning at the end of a unit or course. Both types of assessments serve unique purposes and can be used to improve teaching and learning outcomes. In this article, we will discuss the principles of formative and summative assessments and how they can be used to guide instruction.

Formative Assessment

Formative assessment is a process of gathering evidence of student learning throughout the instructional process. It is designed to monitor student progress and provide immediate feedback to students, so they can adjust their learning strategies to achieve their learning goals. Formative assessment is an ongoing process that helps teachers understand how well their students are learning, and make adjustments to their instruction to better meet the needs of their students. Formative assessment can take many forms, including quizzes, exit tickets, observations, discussions, and portfolios.

Principles of Formative Assessment

Clarity of Learning Goals: Formative assessment should be aligned with clear learning goals. The learning goals should be communicated to the students, and the assessment should be designed to measure progress towards the goals.

Active Involvement: Formative assessment should involve students actively in the learning process. This means that students should be given opportunities to self-assess, peer-assess, and engage in discussions with their peers and teachers about their learning progress.

Immediate Feedback: Formative assessment should provide immediate feedback to students. This allows students to adjust their learning strategies to achieve their learning goals. Teachers should use the feedback to adjust their instruction to better meet the needs of their students.

Multiple Forms: Formative assessment should take multiple forms. This allows teachers to gather a more comprehensive picture of student learning. Teachers should use a variety of assessment techniques, including written tests, performance assessments, observations, and discussions.

Inclusive: Formative assessment should be inclusive of all students. This means that the assessment should be designed to accommodate the diverse learning needs of the students.

Benefits of Formative Assessment

Promotes Active Learning: Formative assessment promotes active learning by involving students in the learning process. It encourages students to take ownership of their learning and to develop metacognitive skills.

Improves Student Achievement: Formative assessment can improve student achievement by providing immediate feedback and allowing students to adjust their learning strategies.

Supports Differentiated Instruction: Formative assessment can support differentiated instruction by providing teachers with information about the diverse learning needs of their students.

Facilitates Communication: Formative assessment facilitates communication between teachers and students. It allows teachers to provide feedback to students and to adjust their instruction to better meet the needs of their students.

Summative Assessment

Summative assessment is an evaluation of student learning at the end of a unit or course. It is designed to measure student achievement and determine the extent to which students have achieved the learning goals. Summative assessment can take many forms, including standardized tests, final exams, projects, and performance assessments.

Principles of Summative Assessment

Clarity of Learning Goals: Summative assessment should be aligned with clear learning goals. The learning goals should be communicated to the students, and the assessment should be designed to measure progress towards the goals.

Validity: Summative assessment should be valid. This means that the assessment should measure what it is intended to measure. The assessment should be designed to measure student achievement of the learning goals.

Reliability: Summative assessment should be reliable. This means that the assessment should produce consistent results over time. The assessment should be designed to minimize errors and to provide a fair and accurate measure of student achievement.

Objectivity: Summative assessment should be objective. This means that the assessment should be free from bias and subjectivity. The assessment should be based on clear criteria and standards, and the scoring should be consistent across different evaluators.

Authenticity: Summative assessment should be authentic. This means that the assessment should reflect real-world skills and knowledge. The assessment should be designed to measure student achievement of skills and knowledge that are relevant and important to their future success.

Benefits of Summative Assessment

Provides Accountability: Summative assessment provides accountability for student learning. It allows teachers, students, parents, and administrators to evaluate student achievement and to make informed decisions about future learning goals and plans.

Provides Feedback: Summative assessment provides feedback to students about their learning progress. It allows students to reflect on their learning and to identify areas for improvement.

Provides Opportunities for Recognition: Summative assessment provides opportunities for recognition and reward for student achievement. It allows students to showcase their skills and knowledge and to receive recognition for their hard work and dedication.

Encourages Quality Instruction: Summative assessment encourages quality instruction by providing teachers with feedback about the effectiveness of their teaching strategies. It allows teachers to identify areas where they need to improve their instruction and to make adjustments to better meet the needs of their students.

Using Formative and Summative Assessments to Guide Instruction

Formative and summative assessments can be used together to guide instruction and improve student learning outcomes. Here are some strategies for using formative and summative assessments to guide instruction:

Use formative assessments to monitor student progress and adjust instruction: Formative assessments can be used to identify areas where students are struggling and to adjust instruction to better meet their needs. Teachers can use formative assessments to identify students who need additional support and to provide targeted interventions to help them succeed.

Use summative assessments to evaluate student achievement and provide feedback: Summative assessments can be used to evaluate student achievement and to provide feedback to students about their learning progress. Teachers can use summative assessments to identify areas where students need to improve and to provide targeted feedback to help them achieve their learning goals.

Use both formative and summative assessments to inform instruction: Teachers can use both formative and summative assessments to inform their instruction. By analyzing student performance on formative assessments, teachers can identify areas where students need additional instruction and adjust their teaching strategies accordingly. By analyzing student performance on summative assessments, teachers can evaluate the effectiveness of their teaching strategies and make adjustments to improve student learning outcomes.

Involve students in the assessment process: Involve students in the assessment process by providing them with opportunities to self-assess, peer-assess, and reflect on their learning progress. This encourages students to take ownership of their learning and to develop metacognitive skills.

Formative and summative assessments are critical components of the teaching and learning process. Formative assessments are used to monitor student progress throughout the instructional process and provide immediate feedback to students, while summative assessments are used to evaluate student achievement at the end of a unit or course. Both types of assessments can be used to guide instruction and improve student learning outcomes. By using formative and summative assessments together, teachers can identify areas where students need additional support, provide targeted interventions, and adjust their teaching strategies to better meet the needs of their students.

Adapting assessments to meet individual student needs

Assessment is an essential component of education as it provides educators with a measure of student learning and allows them to identify areas of strength and areas that need improvement. It is important for educators to adapt assessments to meet the individual needs of their students to ensure that all students are given the opportunity to demonstrate their knowledge and skills. Adapting assessments can be a complex process, but it is essential to ensure that all students are provided with an equal opportunity to demonstrate their knowledge and skills. In this article, we will explore the importance of adapting assessments to meet individual student needs and provide strategies for doing so effectively.

Why Adapt Assessments?

Adapting assessments is essential because every student is unique and has different needs, strengths, and weaknesses. It is important to ensure that assessments are fair and that they provide an accurate measure of student learning. Adapting assessments can help to reduce barriers to learning and ensure that students are not disadvantaged due to differences in learning styles, ability levels, or disabilities.

Adapting assessments can also help to motivate students and increase their engagement in the learning process. When students feel that the assessment is fair and that they are being assessed on their actual knowledge and skills, they are more likely to be motivated to engage with the material and strive to do their best.

Strategies for Adapting Assessments

Use Universal Design for Learning (UDL) Principles

Universal Design for Learning (UDL) is an approach to education that recognizes that students learn in different ways and that instruction should be designed to meet the needs of all learners. UDL principles can be applied to assessments by providing multiple ways for students to demonstrate their knowledge and skills.

For example, instead of only offering a written test, teachers can provide options such as oral presentations, visual projects, or demonstrations to accommodate different learning styles and abilities. This approach can reduce the impact of learning disabilities and help to engage all students in the assessment process.

Modify Test Administration

Modifying the administration of an assessment can help to ensure that all students are given the opportunity to demonstrate their knowledge and skills. For example, students with visual impairments may require large print or braille versions of the assessment, while students with hearing impairments may require a sign language interpreter.

Additionally, some students may require additional time to complete the assessment due to a learning disability or other accommodations. By providing accommodations for test administration, educators can ensure that all students are given an equal opportunity to demonstrate their knowledge and skills.

Adjust Assessment Content

Another strategy for adapting assessments is to adjust the content to meet individual student needs. For example, students with reading difficulties may require simplified text or graphic organizers to help them understand the content. Alternatively, students with a stronger visual-spatial intelligence may benefit from more visually-oriented assessments.

It is important to note that adjusting the content should not change the level of difficulty or the assessment's rigor. Rather, the focus should be on making the assessment accessible to all students while still measuring their knowledge and skills accurately.

Provide Rubrics and Clear Guidelines

Providing rubrics and clear guidelines can help to ensure that all students understand what is expected of them on an assessment. Rubrics provide a clear structure for grading and allow students to understand what they need to do to demonstrate proficiency.

Clear guidelines can also help to reduce anxiety and confusion about what is being assessed. When students understand the assessment criteria and what is expected of them, they are more likely to be able to demonstrate their knowledge and skills accurately.

Use Authentic Assessments

Authentic assessments are assessments that are designed to measure real-world skills and knowledge. These assessments can help to increase student engagement and motivation as they are often more relevant to students' lives and interests.

Authentic assessments can take many forms, such as creating a project or solving a real-world problem. By using authentic assessments, educators can also provide opportunities for students to demonstrate their knowledge and skills in a way that is meaningful and applicable to their lives.

Provide Feedback and Opportunities for Improvement

Providing feedback and opportunities for improvement is essential for adapting assessments to meet individual student needs. Feedback should be timely, specific, and actionable, providing students with clear guidance on how to improve their performance.

Additionally, providing opportunities for improvement allows students to demonstrate their knowledge and skills over time, rather than just on a single assessment. This approach can help to reduce the impact of one-time assessment scores on students' overall grades and provide a more accurate measure of their learning.

Collaborate with Colleagues and Families

Collaborating with colleagues and families can also be an effective strategy for adapting assessments to meet individual student needs. Educators can work with other teachers or specialists to develop assessments that are tailored to specific student needs, such as English language learners or students with disabilities.

Additionally, involving families in the assessment process can provide valuable insights into students' strengths and weaknesses and can help to identify areas for improvement. This collaborative approach can help to ensure that all students are provided with the support they need to succeed.

Adapting assessments to meet individual student needs is essential for ensuring that all students are given an equal opportunity to demonstrate their knowledge and skills. By using strategies such as Universal Design for Learning (UDL) principles, modifying test administration, adjusting assessment content, providing rubrics and clear guidelines, using authentic assessments, providing feedback and opportunities for improvement, and collaborating with colleagues and families, educators can provide a more accurate measure of student learning and ensure that all students are engaged and motivated in the learning process.

Addressing language and cultural differences in assessment

Assessment is an important aspect of the education process, and it is critical that it is conducted in a way that is inclusive and equitable for all students, regardless of their language or cultural background. In this article, we will discuss strategies for addressing language and cultural differences in assessment.

Understanding Language and Cultural Differences

The first step in addressing language and cultural differences in assessment is to understand the ways in which these differences can impact student performance. Language differences can affect a student's ability to understand and respond to test questions, particularly if the student is not fluent in the language of instruction. Cultural differences can also impact performance, as different cultural backgrounds may have different expectations and approaches to learning and assessment.

Assessment Strategies for Addressing Language and Cultural Differences

Use Multiple Assessment Methods

Using multiple assessment methods can help to ensure that all students are able to demonstrate their knowledge and skills. For example, teachers can use both written and oral assessments, or provide opportunities for students to demonstrate their knowledge through creative projects or performance tasks.

Use Multilingual Assessments

Providing assessments in multiple languages can help to ensure that students who are not fluent in the language of instruction are able to demonstrate their knowledge and skills. This can include providing assessments in students' home languages or providing translations of assessment materials.

Provide Accommodations

Providing accommodations can help to level the playing field for students with language or cultural differences. For example, teachers can provide extra time for students who need it, or provide translations of test instructions.

Use Culturally Responsive Assessments

Culturally responsive assessments take into account the cultural background of the student and are designed to be more inclusive and relevant to their experiences. This can include using examples and scenarios that are familiar to the student, or using assessments that are based on real-world situations.

Use Universal Design for Learning (UDL) Principles

UDL principles emphasize the importance of designing assessments that are accessible to all learners. This can include using multiple modes of representation, providing multiple means of expression, and providing multiple means of engagement.

Provide Clear and Explicit Instructions

Providing clear and explicit instructions can help to ensure that all students understand what is expected of them on the assessment. This can include providing examples of what a high-quality response looks like, or breaking down complex tasks into smaller, more manageable steps.

Build Relationships with Students

Building relationships with students can help to create a safe and supportive learning environment where students feel comfortable taking risks and demonstrating their knowledge and skills. This can include taking the time to get to know each student, showing empathy and understanding, and providing positive feedback and support.

Addressing language and cultural differences in assessment is essential for ensuring that all students are given an equal opportunity to demonstrate their knowledge and skills. By using strategies such as using multiple assessment methods, providing multilingual assessments, providing accommodations, using culturally responsive assessments, using UDL principles, providing clear and explicit instructions, and building relationships with students, educators can create an inclusive and equitable assessment environment that supports all learners.

CHAPTER 5

DIFFERENTIATING INSTRUCTION IN LITERACY

Differentiating instruction in reading and writing is essential for meeting the diverse needs of students. In a classroom, students vary in their literacy skills, experiences, interests, and learning preferences. Teachers need to use a range of instructional strategies and materials to provide multiple pathways to learning, so that all students can progress and achieve success in reading and writing. In this article, we will discuss strategies for differentiating instruction in reading and writing.

Assessment and Data Analysis

Effective differentiation in reading and writing instruction begins with assessing student's current levels of reading and writing achievement. This can be done through formal assessments, such as standardized tests, or informal assessments, such as observations, reading conferences, and writing conferences. Teachers can use this data to group students based on their needs and strengths, and tailor instruction to individual or small groups of students.

Flexible Grouping

Flexible grouping is a key strategy for differentiating instruction in reading and writing. Teachers can create small groups of students who share similar reading or writing needs or interests, and provide instruction that is targeted to their needs. For example, struggling readers may benefit from working in a group focused on phonics and decoding, while advanced readers may benefit from working in a group focused on comprehension and analysis. Similarly, students who struggle with writing may benefit from working in a small group to focus on specific skills such as organization, word choice, or revising and editing.

Choice and Interest-Based Learning

Giving students choice and incorporating their interests into reading and writing activities can increase engagement and motivation. For example, allowing students to choose their own books to read, or giving them options for writing prompts, can help them to take ownership of their learning and feel invested in their progress.

Leveled Reading Materials

Providing students with leveled reading materials is an effective way to differentiate instruction. Leveled books are categorized according to a student's reading level, and can help to ensure that students are reading materials that are appropriate for their abilities. Teachers can use these materials to create reading groups, or provide individualized instruction based on a student's needs.

Graphic Organizers and Visual Aids

Graphic organizers and visual aids can help students to understand and remember key concepts and ideas in reading and writing. Teachers can use graphic organizers to help students organize their thoughts before writing, or to visually represent concepts such as plot, character, and theme in literature. Similarly, visual aids such as diagrams, charts, and images can help students to better understand and remember information.

Technology-Based Instruction

Technology can provide a variety of ways to differentiate reading and writing instruction. For example, teachers can use educational software and online resources to provide students with leveled reading materials, interactive writing prompts, and multimedia tools for creating and sharing written work. Technology can also be used to provide additional support for struggling readers, such as text-to-speech software, or to provide more challenging reading and writing activities for advanced learners.

Differentiated Writing Instruction

Writing instruction can be differentiated in a variety of ways. For example, teachers can provide sentence starters or graphic organizers to help struggling writers organize their thoughts and ideas. Similarly, teachers can provide word banks or vocabulary lists to help students expand their writing skills. Teachers can also differentiate writing instruction by providing different levels of scaffolding or feedback based on individual student needs.

Peer Collaboration

Peer collaboration can be an effective way to differentiate instruction in reading and writing. By working with peers who have similar reading or writing abilities, students can provide support and feedback to each other. Teachers can facilitate peer collaboration by providing opportunities for students to work in pairs or small groups, and by teaching students effective strategies for providing constructive feedback.

Adapting instruction to different literacy levels

Adapting instruction to different literacy levels is a crucial part of effective teaching. Students enter the classroom with varying levels of literacy, ranging from students who have not yet learned to read to those who are reading several grade levels above their peers. Therefore, teachers must employ strategies that are appropriate for the students' level of literacy in order to meet their individual needs.

To begin with, teachers must conduct an assessment of their students' literacy skills at the beginning of the school year or term. This assessment will allow teachers to identify students who are struggling with literacy and those who are reading above their grade level. Based on this assessment, teachers can create a literacy plan that will provide appropriate instruction to each student.

One way to adapt instruction to different literacy levels is through the use of leveled books. Leveled books are books that are written at different reading levels. This allows students to read books that are appropriate for their reading level. For example, struggling readers can read books that are written at a lower reading level, while advanced readers can read books that are written at a higher reading level. Teachers can use leveled books to create small reading groups, which allows them to provide targeted instruction to students at each reading level.

Another strategy for adapting instruction to different literacy levels is through the use of graphic organizers. Graphic organizers help students to organize their thoughts and ideas in a visual way. This is particularly helpful for struggling readers

71

who may have difficulty organizing their thoughts when reading and writing. Teachers can use graphic organizers to help struggling readers understand the main ideas of a text or to help them organize their thoughts when writing.

Using technology is another effective way to adapt instruction to different literacy levels. For example, students can use text-to-speech software to listen to a text being read aloud. This can be particularly helpful for struggling readers who may have difficulty reading a text on their own. Similarly, advanced readers can use software that allows them to annotate and highlight text, which can help them to analyze and understand a text at a deeper level.

In addition to these strategies, teachers can use differentiated instruction to meet the needs of students with different literacy levels. Differentiated instruction involves providing different ways of learning for students based on their individual needs. For example, teachers can provide struggling readers with more visual aids, such as pictures and diagrams, to help them understand a text. Advanced readers, on the other hand, may benefit from more challenging reading material or opportunities to engage in higher-level thinking activities.

Ultimately, adapting instruction to different literacy levels requires teachers to be flexible and creative. Teachers must be willing to try different strategies and approaches to help students who are struggling with literacy and to challenge students who are reading above their grade level. By using a variety of strategies and tools, teachers can ensure that all students are receiving instruction that meets their individual needs and helps them to achieve their full potential.

Using technology to support differentiated literacy instruction

Technology has revolutionized education, providing teachers with powerful tools to support differentiated literacy instruction. Differentiated instruction is an approach to teaching that takes into account the diverse needs of students and adapts instruction to meet those needs. In the context of literacy instruction, this means using technology to provide students with individualized support and to help them develop the skills they need to succeed as readers and writers.

One way that technology can support differentiated literacy instruction is through the use of digital texts. Digital texts are electronic versions of books, articles, and other written materials. Digital texts have many advantages over traditional print materials, including the ability to customize the reading experience. For example, digital texts can be formatted to accommodate different reading levels, allowing struggling readers to access content that might otherwise be too difficult for them. Digital texts can also include interactive features such as videos, images, and hyperlinks, which can help to engage students and enhance their understanding of the content.

Another way that technology can support differentiated literacy instruction is through the use of online assessment tools. Online assessment tools allow teachers to evaluate students' literacy skills in real-time and provide immediate feedback. This can be particularly useful for struggling readers who may benefit from additional support and guidance. Online assessment tools can also be used to track students' progress over time, providing teachers with valuable data that can be used to adjust instruction and support students' individual needs.

Technology can also support differentiated literacy instruction through the use of adaptive learning software. Adaptive learning software is designed to adjust instruction based on students' individual needs and progress. For example, some adaptive learning software programs use algorithms to analyze students' responses to questions and determine which skills they need to work on. The software can then provide students with targeted instruction and practice activities to help them master those skills. This approach is particularly effective for students who are struggling with literacy, as it allows them to receive additional support and practice in areas where they need it most.

Digital storytelling is another powerful tool that can be used to support differentiated literacy instruction. Digital storytelling involves using technology to create multimedia stories, incorporating images, videos, and other elements to create a more engaging and interactive reading experience. Digital storytelling can be a particularly effective way to support struggling readers, as it allows them to engage with content in a more meaningful way. For example, students might create digital stories based on books they have read, incorporating images and videos to help them retell the story and reinforce their understanding of the content.

Finally, technology can support differentiated literacy instruction through the use of social media and other collaborative tools. Social media platforms like Twitter, Instagram, and Facebook can be used to facilitate discussions and promote collaborative learning among students. These platforms can also be used to encourage students to share their work with each other and provide feedback and support. Collaborative tools like Google Docs and Padlet can also be used to create a collaborative learning environment where students can work together to share ideas and build knowledge.

Technology provides powerful tools to support differentiated literacy instruction. By using digital texts, online assessment tools, adaptive learning software, digital storytelling, and collaborative tools, teachers can create a learning environment that meets the diverse needs of their students. By leveraging the power of technology, teachers can help struggling readers to develop the skills they need to succeed, while challenging advanced readers to reach their full potential.

Addressing diverse language needs in literacy instruction

Language is a critical aspect of literacy instruction, as it is the primary medium through which students access and interact with texts. However, many students in today's classrooms come from linguistically diverse backgrounds, and may struggle to access literacy instruction due to language barriers. Addressing diverse language needs in literacy instruction is therefore an essential part of ensuring that all students have access to high-quality literacy education.

One of the key strategies for addressing diverse language needs in literacy instruction is to provide students with opportunities to engage with texts in multiple languages. This can be particularly beneficial for students who are bilingual or multilingual, as it allows them to build on their existing language skills while also developing their literacy skills in English. Providing access to texts in students' home languages can also help to build their confidence and motivation as readers, as they see that their linguistic and cultural backgrounds are valued in the classroom.

Another strategy for addressing diverse language needs in literacy instruction is to use culturally responsive teaching practices. Culturally responsive teaching involves using students' cultural backgrounds and experiences as a foundation for instruction, and adapting instruction to meet the diverse needs of students. This can be particularly important for students who come from culturally and linguistically diverse backgrounds, as it helps to build their sense of identity and connection to the content being studied. Culturally responsive teaching practices can include incorporating cultural references into texts and activities, using students' cultural experiences as a basis for discussion and analysis, and valuing and celebrating students' linguistic and cultural backgrounds.

Another strategy for addressing diverse language needs in literacy instruction is to provide targeted support to students who are struggling with English language proficiency. This can include using English language development strategies such as language modeling, explicit instruction in grammar and vocabulary, and providing opportunities for students to practice their English language skills through reading and writing activities. Providing targeted support to students who are struggling with English language proficiency can help to ensure that they are able to access and engage with literacy instruction at their grade level.

In addition to providing targeted support for students who are struggling with English language proficiency, it is also important to ensure that instruction is differentiated to meet the diverse needs of all students. This can include providing alternative modes of instruction, such as visual aids or hands-on activities, for students who may struggle with reading or writing. It can also include using scaffolding techniques to gradually build students' language and literacy skills, and providing opportunities for students to work in small groups or one-on-one with the teacher to receive individualized support.

Finally, it is important to recognize and address the cultural and linguistic biases that may be present in literacy instruction.

Teachers should be mindful of their own cultural and linguistic assumptions and biases, and work to create a classroom environment that is inclusive and welcoming for all students. This can include providing opportunities for students to share their cultural and linguistic experiences and perspectives, valuing and incorporating diverse cultural and linguistic practices into instruction, and being open to feedback and input from students and families.

Addressing diverse language needs in literacy instruction is essential for ensuring that all students have access to high-quality literacy education. By providing opportunities for students to engage with texts in multiple languages, using culturally responsive teaching practices, providing targeted support for English language proficiency, differentiating instruction to meet the diverse needs of all students, and addressing cultural and linguistic biases, teachers can create a learning environment that is inclusive and supportive of all learners. By valuing and incorporating students' diverse linguistic and cultural backgrounds into literacy instruction, teachers can help to promote equity and academic success for all students.

CHAPTER 6

DIFFERENTIATING INSTRUCTION IN MATH

Mathematics is an important subject that is widely taught in schools around the world. It is also a subject that requires a high level of conceptual understanding, making it challenging for many students. One of the key challenges that math teachers face is how to differentiate instruction to meet the needs of students with varying levels of math ability. In this article, we will explore some strategies that can be used to differentiate instruction in math.

Pre-Assessment

Pre-assessment is a valuable tool for differentiating instruction in math. Before starting a new topic, teachers can use pre-assessment to determine the students' current level of understanding. This information can then be used to group students according to their needs. For example, students who have already mastered a particular concept can be given extension activities while students who need extra help can be given additional support.

Flexible Grouping

Flexible grouping is another effective strategy for differentiating instruction in math. This strategy involves grouping students based on their needs and ability levels, and then providing instruction that is tailored to their individual needs. This can be done through small group instruction, peer tutoring, or one-on-one instruction. Teachers can use data from pre-assessment and ongoing formative assessments to group students effectively.

Choice Boards

Choice boards are a popular strategy for differentiating instruction in math. Choice boards provide students with a range of tasks or activities to choose from, allowing them to work on tasks that are appropriate for their level of understanding. This strategy can be particularly effective for students who are struggling with a particular concept, as it allows them to work on tasks that are designed to support their learning.

Math Centers

Math centers are another effective way to differentiate instruction in math. Math centers are stations that are set up around the classroom, each with a different math activity or task. Students can rotate around the centers, working on tasks that are appropriate for their level of understanding. This strategy can be particularly effective for students who need extra support or for students who need extension activities.

Use of Technology

Technology can be a valuable tool for differentiating instruction in math. There are a range of math software programs and apps available that can be used to provide students with personalized instruction. For example, some programs provide students with interactive tutorials and practice exercises that are tailored to their individual needs. Teachers can use data from these programs to track student progress and adjust instruction accordingly.

Open-Ended Tasks

Open-ended tasks are tasks that have more than one correct answer and require students to apply their knowledge and skills in a creative way. Open-ended tasks can be an effective way to differentiate instruction in math as they allow students to work on tasks that are appropriate for their level of understanding. For example, students who have already mastered a particular concept can be given more complex open-ended tasks, while students who are struggling can be given simpler tasks.

Anchor Activities

Anchor activities are tasks that students can work on independently when they have completed their classwork. Anchor activities can be an effective way to differentiate instruction in math as they provide students with a range of tasks to choose from, allowing them to work on tasks that are appropriate for their level of understanding.

Peer Tutoring

Peer tutoring is an effective way to differentiate instruction in math. Students who have already mastered a particular concept can be paired with students who are struggling, allowing them to work together to support each other's learning. Peer tutoring can also be an effective way to build social skills and promote positive relationships in the classroom.

Adapting instruction to different math levels

Adapting instruction to different math levels can be a challenging task for teachers, as students may have varying levels of understanding and proficiency in math. However, with the right strategies and tools, teachers can effectively differentiate math instruction to meet the needs of all students.

Assess students' math levels: Before beginning any math instruction, it is essential to assess each student's math level. This assessment can include standardized tests, informal assessments, and observations. Based on the assessment results, teachers can group students with similar math levels and tailor instruction to meet their needs.

Use hands-on activities: Hands-on activities are an excellent way to engage students in math instruction and differentiate instruction based on their math levels. For example, teachers can use manipulatives such as blocks, counters, and base ten blocks to help students visualize math concepts.

Provide multiple ways of learning: Not all students learn the same way, so it is essential to provide multiple ways of learning to differentiate math instruction. For example, teachers can use visual aids, videos, and audio materials to teach math concepts. They can also provide online resources and interactive activities to allow students to work at their own pace.

Scaffold instruction: Scaffolding is a teaching technique that breaks down complex concepts into smaller, more manageable pieces. Teachers can scaffold math instruction by providing step-by-step instructions and modeling math problems. They can also provide guided practice and feedback to help students build their math skills.

Differentiate homework and assessments: Homework and assessments are an essential part of math instruction. To differentiate instruction, teachers can provide different homework assignments based on the student's math level. They can also provide different versions of assessments based on the student's proficiency level, such as modified or extended assignments.

Use technology: Technology is a powerful tool that can be used to differentiate math instruction. Teachers can use online resources, educational apps, and interactive whiteboards to engage students in math instruction. They can also use adaptive learning software to personalize math instruction based on the student's math level.

Encourage collaboration: Collaborative learning is an effective way to differentiate math instruction. Teachers can group students with different math levels and assign them collaborative math projects. This strategy allows students to learn from each other and build their math skills.

Provide ongoing feedback: Feedback is essential in math instruction. Teachers can provide ongoing feedback to students to help them improve their math skills. Feedback can be provided in the form of comments on homework assignments, assessments, and in-class activities.

Adapting instruction to different math levels can be a challenging task for teachers. However, by assessing students' math levels, providing multiple ways of learning, scaffolding instruction, differentiating homework and assessments, using technology, encouraging collaboration, and providing ongoing feedback, teachers can effectively differentiate math instruction to meet the needs of all students.

Using technology to support differentiated math instruction

Technology has become an integral part of modern education, and it has proven to be an effective tool for differentiated math instruction. Technology can help teachers to tailor math instruction to meet the diverse learning needs of students, provide students with individualized learning experiences, and enhance engagement and motivation. In this article, we will explore how technology can be used to support differentiated math instruction.

Adaptive Learning Software: Adaptive learning software is one of the most effective tools for differentiating math instruction. It uses algorithms to track the progress of each student and adjust the difficulty level of the material accordingly. This way, the software can provide personalized learning experiences based on each student's proficiency level, learning style, and pace. Adaptive learning software can also provide instant feedback and data analytics to help teachers monitor the progress of their students and adjust their instruction as needed.

Online Math Games: Online math games are a fun and interactive way to engage students in math instruction. They can help students practice math concepts in a fun and engaging way. Teachers can assign different math games based on the student's proficiency level, and they can use data analytics to track the progress of each student. Some popular online math games include Math Playground, Coolmath Games, and Hooda Math.

Educational Apps: Educational apps are another great tool for differentiated math instruction. They provide students with interactive and engaging learning experiences that can be tailored to their individual needs. There are a variety of educational apps available for math instruction, including

Mathletics, Khan Academy, and Mathway. Teachers can use these apps to assign different math problems based on the student's proficiency level, and they can provide feedback and data analytics to monitor their progress.

Interactive Whiteboards: Interactive whiteboards are becoming increasingly popular in classrooms. They provide teachers with a visual tool for teaching math concepts, and they can be used to engage students in interactive math activities. Interactive whiteboards can also be used to differentiate math instruction by allowing teachers to display different math problems based on the student's proficiency level. For example, teachers can display a more complex math problem for advanced students while providing simpler problems for struggling students.

Digital Math Manipulatives: Digital math manipulatives are another tool that can be used to support differentiated math instruction. These are digital versions of physical manipulatives such as blocks, counters, and base ten blocks. They allow students to interact with math concepts in a virtual environment, providing a visual and interactive learning experience. Teachers can use digital math manipulatives to differentiate math instruction by providing different levels of complexity and by allowing students to work at their own pace.

Video Tutorials: Video tutorials are an effective tool for differentiated math instruction, as they provide students with an alternative way of learning math concepts. Teachers can create their own video tutorials, or they can use pre-existing video tutorials available online. Video tutorials can be used to provide additional explanations, demonstrations, or to review previously taught concepts. Teachers can also assign different video tutorials based on the student's proficiency level.

Online Math Worksheets: Online math worksheets are a convenient way to differentiate math instruction. Teachers can use online worksheets to assign different math problems based on the student's proficiency level, and they can provide instant feedback to monitor their progress. Some popular websites that offer online math worksheets include Math-Aids, Math-Drills, and Super Teacher Worksheets.

Technology has become an essential tool for differentiated math instruction. Adaptive learning software, online math games, educational apps, interactive whiteboards, digital math manipulatives, video tutorials, and online math worksheets are just a few examples of how technology can be used to support differentiated math instruction. By using technology in creative ways, teachers can tailor math instruction to meet the diverse learning needs of their students and enhance student engagement and motivation.

Addressing diverse language needs in math instruction

Mathematics is a subject that requires a lot of skills and understanding to be able to solve problems. However, every student comes with a different set of skills, knowledge, and abilities. To be an effective math teacher, it is essential to recognize these differences and provide differentiated instruction that meets each student's individual needs. In addition, students from diverse linguistic backgrounds may also require special attention in the math classroom. This paper will discuss strategies for differentiating instruction in math, adapting instruction to different math levels, using technology to support differentiated math instruction, and addressing diverse language needs in math instruction.

Strategies for Differentiating Instruction in Math

Flexible grouping: This strategy involves grouping students according to their math abilities and needs. For example, a teacher may group students who need additional support in math together to receive extra instruction, while advanced students may be grouped together to work on more challenging tasks.

Tiered instruction: This strategy involves providing different levels of instruction for students at different math levels. For example, a teacher may provide a lower-level worksheet for students who need additional support and a more challenging worksheet for advanced students.

Task differentiation: This strategy involves providing students with different tasks that are appropriate for their math level. For example, a teacher may provide a student who struggles with basic math facts with an activity that focuses on mastering those facts while providing an advanced student with a task that requires more complex problem-solving skills.

Multi-sensory instruction: This strategy involves providing instruction that appeals to all of the senses, including visual, auditory, and kinesthetic. For example, a teacher may use manipulatives, visuals, and songs to teach math concepts.

Adapting Instruction to Different Math Levels

Pre-assessment: Before beginning a math unit, it is essential to pre-assess students to determine their math knowledge and skills. Pre-assessment data can help a teacher plan appropriate instruction that meets each student's needs.

Use of Learning Progressions: A learning progression is a series of steps or stages that students must master to achieve proficiency in a particular subject. By using learning progressions, teachers can identify the knowledge and skills students need to learn at each level and adjust their instruction accordingly.

Scaffolded Instruction: This strategy involves breaking down complex math concepts into smaller, more manageable parts. By doing so, students can build their understanding of the concept incrementally.

Modified Assignments: Teachers can modify math assignments by adjusting the complexity of the problems, reducing the number of problems, or providing additional support to help students complete the task successfully.

Using Technology to Support Differentiated Math Instruction

Online Games: Online games provide an engaging and interactive way to teach math concepts. There are a wide variety of online math games available that can be tailored to meet each student's needs.

Adaptive Software: Adaptive software is designed to adjust the level of difficulty based on a student's performance. This technology can provide personalized instruction that meets each student's individual needs.

Learning Management Systems: Learning management systems provide a platform for teachers to deliver instruction, monitor student progress, and provide feedback. These systems can be used to provide differentiated instruction to each student.

Addressing Diverse Language Needs in Math Instruction

Vocabulary Development: Math vocabulary can be challenging for students who are learning English. Teachers can support these students by explicitly teaching math vocabulary and providing opportunities for students to practice using the terms.

Visual Aids: Visual aids can help students who are struggling with language to understand math concepts. Teachers can use diagrams, graphs, and charts to help these students visualize the math concept.

Cooperative Learning: Cooperative learning provides opportunities for students to work together to solve math problems. This strategy can be particularly effective for students who are learning English because it provides opportunities.

CHAPTER 7

DIFFERENTIATING INSTRUCTION IN SCIENCE

Differentiating instruction is a critical approach to meet the diverse learning needs of students, and it is not limited to language arts and math only. Science instruction can also be differentiated, and it is essential to do so since students have different levels of prior knowledge, skills, interests, and abilities. Differentiated science instruction can promote student engagement, motivation, and learning outcomes. In this article, we will discuss strategies for differentiating instruction in science.

Pre-assessment

Pre-assessment is a critical step in differentiating instruction since it helps identify students' prior knowledge, skills, and misconceptions. Pre-assessment can be formal or informal and can take various forms, such as quizzes, surveys, questionnaires, observations, discussions, and interviews. Pre-assessment data can inform teachers about students' readiness levels and guide the selection of appropriate instructional strategies and materials.

Flexible grouping

Flexible grouping is a strategy that involves grouping students based on their learning needs, interests, and abilities. The groups can be homogeneous or heterogeneous and can change frequently depending on the topic or task. Flexible grouping allows teachers to provide instruction and support that targets students' specific needs, such as remediation, enrichment, or acceleration. It also promotes collaboration, social interaction, and communication skills.

Multiple intelligences

Howard Gardner's theory of multiple intelligences proposes that students have diverse intelligences, such as linguistic, logical-mathematical, spatial, bodily-kinesthetic, musical, interpersonal, and intrapersonal. Teachers can use multiple intelligences to differentiate instruction by designing activities that cater to students' preferred intelligences. For example, teachers can provide visual aids, hands-on activities, and music to enhance students' learning experiences and engagement.

Tiered assignments

Tiered assignments are tasks that have different levels of complexity, depth, and abstractness, but they address the same essential concept or skill. Tiered assignments allow teachers to provide appropriate challenges and support for students with different readiness levels. Teachers can create tiered assignments by modifying the tasks' content, process, product, or outcome. For example, a tiered assignment on the water cycle can have three levels: basic, intermediate, and advanced. The basic level could be labeling the water cycle diagram, the intermediate level could be explaining the water cycle's stages, and the advanced level could be creating a model that demonstrates the water cycle.

Learning stations

Learning stations are a strategy that involves dividing the classroom into various stations or centers, each with a different activity or task. Learning stations allow students to work independently or collaboratively, depending on their needs and interests. Teachers can design learning stations that target different learning styles, multiple intelligences, and academic levels. For example, a science learning station could have the following centers: reading and summarizing a text, conducting a hands-on experiment, watching a video, and creating a visual aid.

Inquiry-based learning

Inquiry-based learning is a strategy that involves students in the process of asking questions, investigating, and discovering knowledge. Inquiry-based learning allows students to construct their own understanding and meaning of scientific concepts and principles. Teachers can differentiate inquiry-based learning by providing different levels of guidance, structure, and support. For example, students with lower readiness levels can receive more teacher guidance, while students with higher readiness levels can have more autonomy.

Graphic organizers

Graphic organizers are visual tools that help students organize and represent information, concepts, and relationships. Graphic organizers can be used to differentiate instruction by adapting the content and format to students' needs and preferences. For example, teachers can provide graphic organizers that scaffold students' understanding of scientific concepts, such as Venn diagrams, concept maps, and cause-and-effect diagrams.

Use real-world examples and experiences: One effective way to make science more accessible and engaging for all students is to incorporate real-world examples and experiences into the curriculum. This allows students to connect what they are learning in the classroom to their own lives and experiences, making the content more relevant and meaningful. For example, teachers can use local environmental issues to teach science concepts such as pollution, conservation, and ecology. They can also bring in guest speakers from local science organizations or arrange field trips to science-related locations in the community.

Adapting instruction to different science levels

Science is a subject that can be challenging for many students, as it often requires a strong understanding of complex concepts and theories. Therefore, it is important for teachers to adapt their instruction to meet the needs of students at different science levels. In this article, we will discuss some strategies for adapting instruction to different science levels to ensure that all students can engage with and understand the content.

Pre-Assessment: Before starting any unit or lesson, it is important to assess the prior knowledge of your students. This will help you to identify any gaps in their understanding and tailor your instruction accordingly. Pre-assessments can be in the form of quizzes, concept maps, or open-ended questions. Once you have identified the areas where your students need support, you can create a plan to fill those gaps.

Differentiated Instruction: Differentiated instruction is a teaching approach that involves tailoring instruction to meet the needs of individual students. This approach is particularly effective in science as it allows teachers to differentiate instruction based on a student's prior knowledge, interests, learning style, and pace of learning. Some strategies for differentiated instruction in science include tiered assignments, flexible grouping, and using a variety of teaching strategies to engage all students.

Hands-on Activities: Science is a subject that requires students to engage in hands-on activities to truly understand the concepts being taught. These activities allow students to see the concepts in action and apply what they have learned. Teachers can use hands-on activities to differentiate instruction by providing different levels of complexity or scaffolding to support students at different science levels.

Small Group Work: Small group work is a great way to differentiate instruction in science. Students can work in small groups based on their ability level, interests, or prior knowledge. Teachers can assign roles within the group to ensure that everyone has a chance to contribute and learn. This strategy can also be used to allow students to work at their own pace and receive targeted support from the teacher or other students.

Flexible Grouping: Flexible grouping is a strategy that allows teachers to group students based on their needs and abilities. Teachers can change groups regularly based on the content being taught or the skills being developed. This allows students to work with different peers and receive targeted instruction and support.

Technology: Technology can be a powerful tool in science instruction as it allows teachers to provide differentiated instruction and resources to their students. Teachers can use online simulations, virtual labs, and interactive activities to engage students and differentiate instruction. Online resources can also provide support to students who need additional practice or enrichment activities.

Real-world Examples and Experiences: Science is a subject that is rooted in the real world. Teachers can use real-world examples and experiences to make science more accessible and engaging for all students. This can include using local environmental issues to teach science concepts or bringing in guest speakers from local science organizations. Teachers can also arrange field trips to science-related locations in the community to provide students with hands-on experiences.

Scaffolding: Scaffolding is a strategy that involves breaking down complex concepts into smaller, more manageable parts. This allows students to build on their prior knowledge and gradually increase their understanding of the concept. Scaffolding can be done through visual aids, graphic organizers, or by breaking down complex vocabulary into simpler terms.

Adapting instruction to different science levels is essential to ensure that all students can engage with and understand the content. By using a combination of strategies, including pre-assessment, differentiated instruction, hands-on activities, small group work, flexible grouping, technology, real-world examples and experiences, and scaffolding, teachers can help all students succeed in science and develop a love for the subject.

Using technology to support differentiated science instruction

Using technology in the classroom is becoming increasingly common and can be a powerful tool to support differentiated science instruction. Technology can provide access to interactive simulations, videos, virtual labs, and online resources that can enhance students' learning experiences and support differentiated instruction. Here are some examples of how technology can be used to support differentiated science instruction:

Interactive simulations and virtual labs: Many online resources provide interactive simulations and virtual labs that can help students visualize scientific concepts and processes. These resources can be particularly useful for students who may struggle with abstract or complex concepts. For example, the virtual lab "PhET Interactive Simulations" provides a range of interactive simulations that can help students understand complex scientific concepts in physics, chemistry, biology, and earth science.

Adaptive learning platforms: Adaptive learning platforms are online tools that use data analytics and algorithms to personalize learning for each student based on their individual strengths and weaknesses. These platforms can provide tailored instruction and practice activities that are specifically designed to address each student's needs. For example, the platform "Knewton" uses machine learning to provide personalized learning paths for each student.

Multimedia resources: Multimedia resources, such as videos and animations, can help students learn science concepts by providing visual representations and demonstrations of abstract ideas. These resources can be particularly useful for students who are visual or auditory learners. For example, the "Crash Course" series on YouTube provides engaging and informative videos on a range of science topics.

Online resources and tutorials: There are a wide range of online resources and tutorials available for science topics that can be used to support differentiated instruction. These resources can provide additional practice and support for students who may need extra help with certain topics. For example, the website "Khan Academy" provides a range of science tutorials and practice activities for students of all levels.

Collaborative online tools: Collaborative online tools, such as wikis and discussion forums, can be used to support differentiated instruction by allowing students to work together and share ideas. These tools can be particularly useful for students who may benefit from peer support or who may struggle with independent work. For example, the platform "Padlet" allows students to collaborate on a digital bulletin board and share ideas and resources.

By incorporating technology into science instruction, teachers can provide differentiated instruction and support to meet the needs of all learners. However, it is important to ensure that technology is used appropriately and that students are provided with clear guidance and expectations for their use. Teachers should also regularly evaluate the effectiveness of the technology-based instruction and adjust their approach as necessary.

Addressing diverse language needs in science instruction

Science instruction can be challenging for students who have limited proficiency in the language of instruction. Students who are not fluent in the language of instruction may struggle to understand the concepts being taught, which can lead to a lack of engagement and poor academic performance. Therefore, it is important for teachers to address the diverse language needs of their students to ensure that they can fully participate in the learning process.

Here are some strategies for addressing diverse language needs in science instruction:

Use visuals: Using visuals such as diagrams, pictures, and charts can help students who are struggling with the language of instruction. Visual aids can help students understand complex scientific concepts and provide a means for non-verbal communication.

Provide written instructions: Providing written instructions can help students who have difficulty understanding verbal instructions. Written instructions can be used in conjunction with verbal instructions to reinforce learning and to provide a reference for students to use during independent work.

Simplify language: Simplifying language can help students who are struggling with complex scientific terms and concepts. Teachers can use simpler language to explain scientific concepts and gradually introduce more complex terminology as students become more familiar with the concepts.

Use graphic organizers: Graphic organizers such as concept maps and Venn diagrams can help students understand the relationships between different scientific concepts. Graphic organizers can also provide a visual representation of the connections between different scientific concepts.

Encourage group work: Group work can help students who are struggling with the language of instruction by providing an opportunity for peer support. Students can work together to explain concepts and help each other understand difficult vocabulary.

Use technology: Technology can provide a means for students to engage with scientific concepts in a way that is accessible and engaging. Teachers can use online simulations, videos, and interactive resources to help students understand scientific concepts and develop their language skills.

Provide scaffolding: Scaffolding refers to the support that teachers provide to help students understand new concepts. Teachers can provide scaffolding by breaking down complex scientific concepts into smaller, more manageable components, and providing support as students work through each component.

Build vocabulary: Building scientific vocabulary is essential for students to understand the concepts being taught. Teachers can provide students with a list of key scientific terms and encourage students to use these terms in their writing and discussions.

Use real-world examples: Using real-world examples can help students connect scientific concepts to their own experiences. Teachers can use examples from students' own communities to help them understand scientific concepts in a more meaningful way.

Encourage reflection: Encouraging reflection can help students develop their language skills by giving them an opportunity to think about and express their understanding of scientific concepts. Teachers can provide students with prompts for reflection and encourage them to share their reflections with their peers.

Addressing the diverse language needs of students in science instruction is essential to ensure that all students have access to the learning process. Teachers can use a variety of strategies to support students who are struggling with the language of instruction, including using visuals, providing written instructions, simplifying language, using graphic organizers, encouraging group work, using technology, providing scaffolding, building vocabulary, using real-world examples, and encouraging reflection. By addressing the diverse language needs of their students, teachers can help all students engage with scientific concepts and develop their language skills.

CHAPTER 8

DIFFERENTIATING INSTRUCTION IN SOCIAL STUDIES

S ocial studies is a subject that encompasses a wide range of topics, including history, geography, economics, and political science. Due to the varied nature of the subject, differentiating instruction in social studies can be a challenging task. However, with the right strategies in place, teachers can effectively meet the diverse learning needs of their students. Here are some strategies for differentiating instruction in social studies:

Pre-assessment

Pre-assessment is an effective way to differentiate instruction in social studies. It allows teachers to identify the individual strengths and weaknesses of each student and helps them to tailor their instruction accordingly. Before starting a unit, teachers can administer a pre-assessment to gauge the prior knowledge of their students. Based on the results of the pre-assessment, teachers can identify students who require additional support and those who are ready for more advanced content.

Flexible grouping

Flexible grouping is another effective strategy for differentiating instruction in social studies. It involves grouping students based on their learning needs and abilities. Teachers can create groups based on the results of pre-assessments or observations of student performance. Grouping students flexibly allows teachers to target instruction to meet the specific needs of each group. For example, students who require additional support can be grouped together for more focused instruction, while advanced learners can be challenged with more complex tasks.

Varied instructional strategies

Varied instructional strategies can help teachers differentiate instruction in social studies. Different students have different learning styles, and using a variety of instructional strategies can help reach all learners. Teachers can use a mix of lectures, discussions, debates, simulations, and project-based learning to engage their students. This approach provides opportunities for students to learn through different modes of instruction and appeals to different learning styles.

Tiered assignments

Tiered assignments are an effective way to differentiate instruction in social studies. It involves providing students with different levels of tasks based on their readiness and learning needs. Teachers can design assignments that are aligned with the same learning objectives but vary in complexity, depth, and resources. For example, a tiered assignment on the Civil War could include a basic level that involves identifying key events and people, an intermediate level that requires analyzing the causes and effects of the war, and an advanced level that involves researching and presenting a project on a related topic.

Technology integration

Integrating technology into social studies instruction can be an effective way to differentiate instruction. Technology provides students with opportunities to access information and resources at their own pace and level. Teachers can use online resources, videos, podcasts, and interactive simulations to engage their students and support their learning. This approach allows students to work at their own pace, explore different topics in depth, and receive feedback on their progress.

Inquiry-based learning

Inquiry-based learning is a student-centered approach to teaching that involves posing questions and problems and encouraging students to investigate and find solutions. This approach provides opportunities for students to explore different topics and develop critical thinking skills. Teachers can differentiate instruction in social studies by using inquiry-based learning. They can pose open-ended questions that require students to analyze, evaluate, and synthesize information from various sources. This approach allows students to pursue their interests and learning styles while meeting the same learning objectives.

Graphic organizers

Graphic organizers can be an effective tool for differentiating instruction in social studies. They help students to organize their thoughts and ideas and make connections between different concepts. Teachers can use graphic organizers to support students who struggle with reading and writing, to differentiate instruction for different learning styles, and to provide scaffolding for complex tasks. For example, teachers can provide visual organizers for students to use when analyzing primary sources, creating timelines, or comparing and contrasting events.

Adapting instruction to different social studies levels

Adapting instruction to different levels of social studies is essential to ensure that every student gets a chance to learn at their own pace and at their level of understanding. In social studies, students learn about history, geography, economics, government, and culture. It is crucial for teachers to differentiate instruction based on students' needs and abilities to help them achieve success in social studies. Below are some strategies for adapting instruction to different levels in social studies.

Pre-Assessment: Before starting any new topic or lesson, the teacher can conduct a pre-assessment to determine the students' prior knowledge and understanding of the topic. This will help the teacher differentiate instruction by grouping students according to their level of understanding.

Tiered Assignments: Tiered assignments are tasks that vary in difficulty, allowing students to work at their own level of understanding. The teacher can differentiate assignments by providing different tasks to students based on their ability level. For example, a teacher can provide three different reading levels on the same topic and ask students to answer questions related to the reading material. Students can choose the reading level that matches their ability and understanding.

Learning Stations: Learning stations can be set up around the classroom to help differentiate instruction. The teacher can set up different stations with various activities that cater to different learning styles and abilities. For example, one station can be a reading station, where students can read about a specific topic, while another station can be an audio station, where students can listen to a recording related to the topic.

Graphic Organizers: Graphic organizers are visual tools that help students organize their thoughts and ideas. Teachers can provide different graphic organizers for students to use based on their level of understanding. For example, some students may need a simple graphic organizer with fewer details, while others may require a more complex one with more details.

Differentiated Instructional Materials: Teachers can differentiate instruction by using different instructional materials based on students' needs and abilities. For example, the teacher can provide different textbooks, articles, and videos on the same topic, but at different levels of difficulty. This will allow students to learn at their own pace and level of understanding.

Small Group Instruction: Small group instruction allows the teacher to work closely with a group of students who need extra support or extension activities. The teacher can group students based on their level of understanding and provide targeted instruction to meet their needs.

Peer Tutoring: Peer tutoring is an effective way to differentiate instruction in social studies. The teacher can pair students with different abilities and have them work together to complete tasks and activities related to the topic. This will allow students to learn from each other and build confidence.

Technology: Technology can be used to differentiate instruction in social studies. For example, the teacher can provide students with access to different online resources, such as interactive games, videos, and simulations, that cater to different learning styles and abilities. Students can choose the resources that match their level of understanding and learning style.

Adapting instruction to different levels in social studies is crucial to ensure that every student gets a chance to learn at their own pace and at their level of understanding. Teachers can differentiate instruction by using pre-assessments, tiered assignments, learning stations, graphic organizers, differentiated instructional materials, small group instruction, peer tutoring, and technology. By using these strategies, teachers can create a supportive learning environment that caters to the needs and abilities of all students.

Using technology to support differentiated social studies instruction

Using technology to support differentiated instruction in social studies can be a powerful tool for reaching all students, regardless of their skill level or learning style. Here are some strategies for using technology to support differentiated social studies instruction:

Digital Texts: Provide students with digital texts that are adapted to their reading level. This can be achieved through the use of e-books, websites, and online databases that offer leveled texts. Additionally, many digital texts offer multimedia features such as videos and images that can help students better understand complex concepts.

Audio and Video Resources: Using audio and video resources can help to support students who struggle with reading or those who are visual or auditory learners. Teachers can provide students with video lectures, podcasts, or other audiovisual resources that align with the curriculum and can be accessed at the students' pace.

Interactive Learning Activities: Interactive learning activities such as simulations, games, and virtual field trips can provide students with an immersive and engaging learning experience. These activities can also be adapted to meet the needs of different learners, offering differentiated levels of difficulty and pace.

Social Media and Blogging: Encourage students to use social media and blogging platforms to share their perspectives, thoughts, and ideas about social studies topics. These platforms provide a space for students to engage in discussions, connect with peers, and share their learning with a broader audience.

Digital Portfolios: Digital portfolios can be used to showcase student learning and progress over time. They can include a range of different types of media such as images, videos, written work, and multimedia projects. Digital portfolios can be personalized to meet the needs of individual learners, allowing them to highlight their strengths and accomplishments.

Learning Management Systems: A learning management system (LMS) can be used to support differentiated instruction in social studies. An LMS can provide students with access to digital resources and learning activities, allow them to track their progress, and provide teachers with data on student performance. An LMS can also be used to deliver assessments that are tailored to individual student needs.

Virtual Collaboration Tools: Virtual collaboration tools such as video conferencing, chat rooms, and collaborative document editors can be used to facilitate communication and collaboration among students. These tools can provide students with opportunities to work together on social studies projects and share their learning with others.

By utilizing these strategies, teachers can effectively differentiate instruction in social studies and support the diverse needs of their students. Technology can be a powerful tool for promoting engagement, increasing accessibility, and fostering deeper learning in social studies.

Addressing diverse language needs in social studies instruction

Social studies instruction involves the study of history, geography, economics, and politics. These subjects are important for students to learn, as they provide an understanding of the world around them and the forces that shape it. However, social studies instruction can be challenging for students who are learning a new language or who come from different cultural backgrounds. In this article, we will discuss strategies for addressing diverse language needs in social studies instruction.

Use visuals and graphic organizers

Visual aids can be an effective way to support students who are learning a new language. Pictures, diagrams, maps, and charts can help to clarify abstract concepts and vocabulary. Graphic organizers such as mind maps and flowcharts can also be useful for organizing information and helping students to make connections between ideas.

Provide background knowledge

Students who are learning a new language may struggle to understand social studies concepts because they lack the necessary background knowledge. Providing background knowledge can help to bridge this gap. Teachers can introduce new concepts by relating them to students' prior experiences or by using familiar examples.

Use scaffolding

Scaffolding is a teaching strategy that involves breaking down complex tasks into smaller, more manageable steps. This can be especially helpful for students who are learning a new language. Teachers can provide support by modeling new skills or concepts, providing prompts or cues, or breaking down instructions into simpler language.

Incorporate real-world experiences

Incorporating real-world experiences can help to engage students and make social studies concepts more relevant. Teachers can use examples from students' lives, such as stories of their families' journeys to the United States, to help illustrate concepts like immigration and cultural diversity.

Use cooperative learning

Cooperative learning is a teaching strategy that involves small groups of students working together on a task. This can be especially helpful for students who are learning a new language, as it provides opportunities for students to practice their language skills in a supportive environment. Teachers can assign roles within the group, such as a note-taker or a summarizer, to help students focus on specific language skills.

Use technology

Technology can be a powerful tool for supporting students who are learning a new language. There are many online resources and applications that can be used to provide additional support for language learners. For example, teachers can use apps that provide translations, offer pronunciation guides, or provide visual aids.

Provide feedback

Providing feedback is an important part of supporting students who are learning a new language. Teachers can provide feedback in a variety of ways, such as through written comments, verbal feedback, or by modeling correct language use. Feedback should be specific and focused on the language skills that students need to develop.

Incorporate cultural awareness

Incorporating cultural awareness is an important part of social studies instruction. Teachers can use examples from different cultures to help students understand how cultural differences shape people's experiences and perspectives. Additionally, teachers can be mindful of their own cultural biases and work to create a classroom environment that is inclusive of all students.

Addressing diverse language needs in social studies instruction requires a variety of strategies. By using visual aids, providing background knowledge, scaffolding, incorporating real-world experiences, using cooperative learning, using technology, providing feedback, and incorporating cultural awareness, teachers can create a supportive environment that allows all students to learn and thrive.

CHAPTER 9

DIFFERENTIATING INSTRUCTION FOR ENGLISH LANGUAGE LEARNERS

E nglish Language Learners (ELLs) are students who are learning English as a second language while also trying to keep up with their academic curriculum. These students may have a variety of language backgrounds and may be at different stages of language acquisition. Understanding the needs of ELLs is crucial for educators to effectively support their academic and linguistic development. In this article, we will explore the various needs of ELLs and strategies to support their learning.

Creating a welcoming environment

The first step in supporting ELLs is creating a welcoming and inclusive environment. ELLs may feel anxious or intimidated in a new environment and may struggle to communicate their needs. Educators can help by greeting students in their native language, using pictures or gestures to convey information, and providing a comfortable and safe learning environment.

Building relationships

Building strong relationships with ELLs and their families is crucial for their academic success. Educators can meet with families to learn about their cultural background, their expectations for their child's education, and any special needs or considerations. This can help educators tailor their instruction and support to meet the needs of individual students.

Assessing language proficiency

Before educators can effectively support ELLs, they must first assess their language proficiency. This can be done through standardized language assessments, informal language assessments, or by observing the student's language skills in the classroom. This information can help educators tailor their instruction to meet the needs of individual students.

Differentiating instruction

Differentiating instruction is a key strategy for supporting ELLs. Educators can modify instruction to meet the needs of ELLs by providing additional visual aids, using simpler language, and breaking down complex concepts into smaller parts. Educators can also provide additional support through peer tutoring, small group instruction, or one-on-one tutoring.

Providing language support

Providing language support is crucial for the academic success of ELLs. Educators can provide language support by providing additional instruction in English language development, providing bilingual support in the student's native language, or using translation software or interpreters to facilitate communication.

Encouraging bilingualism

Encouraging bilingualism is another way to support ELLs. Bilingualism has many cognitive, academic, and social benefits and can help ELLs maintain their cultural identity. Educators can encourage bilingualism by providing instruction in both English and the student's native language, providing access to bilingual resources, and valuing and celebrating the student's language and cultural background.

Promoting cultural awareness

Promoting cultural awareness is important for creating an inclusive learning environment for ELLs. Educators can promote cultural awareness by integrating diverse cultural perspectives into the curriculum, using culturally relevant teaching materials, and encouraging students to share their cultural experiences and perspectives.

Using technology

Technology can be a powerful tool for supporting ELLs. There are many online resources available for English language development, as well as translation software and language learning apps. Educators can also use technology to provide additional visual aids and interactive learning activities to support ELLs.

Understanding the needs of ELLs is crucial for educators to effectively support their academic and linguistic development. Creating a welcoming and inclusive environment, building strong relationships with students and families, assessing language proficiency, differentiating instruction, providing language support, encouraging bilingualism, promoting cultural awareness, and using technology are all strategies that educators can use to support the learning of ELLs. By implementing these strategies, educators can create a positive and inclusive learning environment that supports the academic and linguistic development of all students.

Strategies for differentiating instruction for ELLs

Strategies for differentiating instruction for English Language Learners (ELLs) are essential for providing equitable and inclusive educational opportunities for all students. ELLs come from diverse linguistic, cultural, and academic backgrounds and face unique challenges when learning English and other subjects in the classroom. Differentiating instruction to meet the needs of ELLs requires teachers to consider various factors such as their language proficiency, prior knowledge, cultural background, and learning style. Here are some effective strategies for differentiating instruction for ELLs:

Provide visual aids and graphic organizers: Visual aids and graphic organizers can help ELLs comprehend and remember information more effectively. Teachers can use images, diagrams, charts, and graphs to supplement the text and support ELLs' understanding of new concepts. Graphic organizers such as concept maps, Venn diagrams, and KWL charts can help ELLs organize and clarify their thinking and connect new information to their prior knowledge.

Use hands-on activities and realia: Hands-on activities and realia such as maps, globes, artifacts, and cultural objects can help ELLs connect with the subject matter and enhance their learning experience. These activities can engage ELLs in meaningful and authentic learning opportunities that promote language development and cultural awareness.

Simplify language and use scaffolding techniques: Simplifying language and using scaffolding techniques can help ELLs understand new vocabulary and concepts. Teachers can use simpler sentences, avoid idiomatic expressions, and break down complex concepts into smaller, more manageable parts. Scaffolding techniques such as modeling, guided practice, and feedback can provide ELLs with the necessary support to master new skills and concepts.

Build on prior knowledge: Building on ELLs' prior knowledge can help them make connections between their native language and culture and the new language and culture they are learning. Teachers can use students' prior knowledge as a foundation for new learning and provide opportunities for ELLs to share their experiences and cultural perspectives with the class.

Provide language support: ELLs need explicit instruction in grammar, syntax, and vocabulary to develop their English language proficiency. Teachers can provide language support through explicit language instruction, structured language practice, and opportunities for language production such as discussions, debates, and presentations.

Promote cultural awareness: Promoting cultural awareness can help ELLs feel valued and respected in the classroom and develop a positive self-image. Teachers can use multicultural literature, videos, and other resources to expose ELLs to diverse cultures and promote understanding and appreciation for cultural differences.

Provide individualized feedback and support: Providing individualized feedback and support can help ELLs monitor their progress and improve their performance. Teachers can provide feedback that is specific, timely, and actionable and use differentiated instruction to address the individual needs of ELLs.

Differentiating instruction for ELLs requires a deep understanding of their linguistic, cultural, and academic needs.

By using a combination of strategies such as visual aids, hands-on activities, scaffolding, and language support, teachers can provide ELLs with meaningful and engaging learning experiences that support their language and academic development.

Adapting instruction to different language proficiency levels

Adapting instruction to different language proficiency levels is essential in supporting English Language Learners (ELLs) in their learning. ELLs come from diverse linguistic and cultural backgrounds and have varying levels of proficiency in English. Therefore, teachers need to tailor their instruction to meet the individual needs of their ELLs. In this article, we will explore some strategies for adapting instruction to different language proficiency levels.

Use Visual Aids and Graphic Organizers

Visual aids and graphic organizers can help ELLs better understand complex concepts by providing a visual representation of the content. They can help ELLs identify key information, understand the relationships between ideas, and organize their own thoughts. Visual aids and graphic organizers can be used in various subjects, such as science, social studies, and math, to support ELLs' learning. Teachers can also use pictures, drawings, and diagrams to help ELLs understand new vocabulary words.

Simplify Language

Teachers can simplify their language by using shorter sentences and avoiding complex sentence structures. They can also use simpler words and explain the meaning of new vocabulary words. Teachers can also rephrase their questions to make them easier for ELLs to understand. When giving instructions, teachers can use simple language and demonstrate what they mean. Teachers can also provide a glossary of important terms for ELLs to refer to throughout the lesson.

Provide Opportunities for Interaction

ELLs need opportunities to practice their English language skills, both in speaking and in writing. Teachers can create a supportive classroom environment that encourages ELLs to ask questions, participate in discussions, and collaborate with their peers. Teachers can also pair ELLs with native English speakers or other ELLs who have higher language proficiency levels to encourage interaction and language practice.

Differentiate Assignments

Teachers can differentiate assignments based on ELLs' language proficiency levels. For example, teachers can provide ELLs with simplified reading materials or audio recordings of the reading materials to help them understand the content. Teachers can also modify writing assignments by providing sentence frames or graphic organizers to help ELLs organize their thoughts. Teachers can also adjust the complexity of math problems to match ELLs' language proficiency levels.

Use Technology

Technology can be a powerful tool to support ELLs' learning. Teachers can use online resources, such as interactive games, videos, and simulations, to help ELLs understand complex concepts. Teachers can also use language-learning software, such as Rosetta Stone or Duolingo, to help ELLs improve their English language skills. Additionally, teachers can provide ELLs with online resources, such as vocabulary flashcards or interactive quizzes, to help them practice and reinforce their learning.

Adapting instruction to different language proficiency levels is crucial in supporting ELLs' learning. Teachers can use visual aids and graphic organizers, simplify language, provide opportunities for interaction, differentiate assignments, and use technology to support ELLs' learning. By adapting instruction to meet the needs of ELLs, teachers can help them succeed academically and socially.

Supporting ELLs in content areas

Supporting English Language Learners (ELLs) in content areas is an important aspect of providing a quality education for all students. ELLs face unique challenges in academic settings because they are still developing their English language skills, which can make it difficult to access and understand content material. However, with the right support, ELLs can successfully participate in content area instruction and achieve academic success.

One of the most effective strategies for supporting ELLs in content areas is to provide them with additional language support. This may include pre-teaching vocabulary, providing simplified instructions or lectures, and using visual aids such as pictures or diagrams to help explain concepts. It is also helpful to incorporate opportunities for ELLs to use their home language, either in small group or individual settings, to help clarify their understanding of content material.

Another effective strategy is to incorporate cultural relevance and sensitivity into content area instruction. ELLs come from diverse cultural and linguistic backgrounds, and incorporating cultural references and examples that are relevant to their experiences can help make the content material more accessible and engaging. Additionally, creating a classroom environment that is welcoming and inclusive can help build a sense of community and support for ELLs.

Collaboration between content area teachers and English language development (ELD) specialists is also key to supporting ELLs in content areas. ELD specialists can provide additional support for ELLs, such as language assessments, specialized language instruction, and resources for teachers to use in their content area instruction. Collaborating with ELD specialists can help teachers better understand the language needs of ELLs and provide them with the necessary support to be successful in content area instruction.

Finally, it is important to recognize the individual needs and strengths of ELLs. Some ELLs may have had more exposure to English and be able to participate in content area instruction more readily, while others may require additional language support. Providing differentiated instruction and accommodations based on individual student needs can help ensure that all ELLs are able to access and understand content area material.

CHAPTER 10

DIFFERENTIATING INSTRUCTION FOR GIFTED AND TALENTED LEARNERS

Gifted and talented learners are students who demonstrate exceptional abilities in one or more areas, such as intellectual, creative, artistic, or leadership skills. These students have unique educational needs and require differentiated instruction to ensure that they reach their full potential. Understanding the needs of gifted and talented learners is essential for educators to provide appropriate instructional strategies and support to these students.

Identification of Gifted and Talented Learners

The identification of gifted and talented learners is typically based on various criteria, including standardized tests, academic performance, creativity, leadership, and artistic talent. Different schools and districts have their own identification procedures and criteria, but most commonly used are IQ tests, academic assessments, and teacher and parent nominations.

Characteristics of Gifted and Talented Learners

Gifted and talented learners often exhibit the following characteristics:

High levels of curiosity and interest in learning new things

Excellent memory and retention abilities

Strong critical thinking and problem-solving skills

Advanced language abilities, including verbal and written communication

High levels of creativity and imagination

Ability to learn and process information quickly

Strong leadership and decision-making skills

Challenges Faced by Gifted and Talented Learners

Gifted and talented learners may face various challenges that can affect their learning and development. Some of the challenges include:

Boredom and disengagement due to the lack of challenging and stimulating learning opportunities

Perfectionism and self-imposed pressure to excel in all areas

Social isolation and difficulty in forming relationships with peers who may not share similar interests or abilities

Imposter syndrome and feeling like they do not belong or are not deserving of their accomplishments

Strategies for Differentiating Instruction for Gifted and Talented Learners

Differentiated instruction is essential for meeting the needs of gifted and talented learners. Here are some strategies that educators can use to differentiate instruction for these students:

Provide challenging and stimulating learning opportunities: Gifted and talented learners thrive in environments that challenge them to think critically and creatively. Teachers can provide opportunities for advanced coursework, independent research projects, and inquiry-based learning activities to keep these students engaged and motivated.

Offer flexible pacing and learning paths: Gifted and talented learners often learn at a faster pace than their peers. Teachers can provide flexible pacing and learning paths, such as allowing students to work at their own pace or providing advanced learning materials and resources.

Use higher-order thinking and problem-solving activities: Gifted and talented learners excel in complex problem-solving activities that require higher-order thinking skills. Teachers can provide opportunities for these students to work on open-ended problems, real-world scenarios, and project-based learning activities.

Encourage collaboration and peer mentoring: Gifted and talented learners benefit from working with their peers who share similar interests and abilities. Teachers can encourage collaboration and peer mentoring activities, such as group projects or peer tutoring.

Provide opportunities for self-directed learning: Gifted and talented learners often have a strong desire to learn independently. Teachers can provide opportunities for self-directed learning, such as independent research projects or independent study courses.

Use technology to support learning: Technology can be an effective tool for providing differentiated instruction to gifted and talented learners. Teachers can use online resources and tools, such as online courses, webinars, and simulations, to provide challenging and engaging learning opportunities.

Gifted and talented learners have unique educational needs that require differentiated instruction to ensure that they reach their full potential. Educators can use various strategies to differentiate instruction for these students, including providing challenging and stimulating learning opportunities, flexible pacing and learning paths, higher-order thinking and problem-solving activities, collaboration and peer mentoring, self-directed learning, and technology-supported learning. By understanding the needs of gifted and talented learners, educators can provide

Strategies for differentiating instruction for gifted and talented learners

Gifted and talented learners are those who demonstrate high levels of intellectual, academic, creative, or artistic ability compared to their peers. These learners often need differentiated instruction to challenge and engage them in meaningful ways. In this article, we will explore strategies for differentiating instruction for gifted and talented learners.

Curriculum Compacting

Curriculum compacting is a strategy that involves identifying the learning objectives that gifted and talented students have already mastered and then allowing them to skip or move through that content more quickly. This allows for more time to be spent on new material that will challenge and engage these learners. The teacher can use pre-assessments to determine which students have already mastered the learning objectives and then create individualized learning plans that are tailored to each student's needs.

Tiered Assignments

Tiered assignments are another way to differentiate instruction for gifted and talented learners. This strategy involves creating assignments that are designed to meet the needs of learners at different levels of proficiency. For example, a teacher may create three versions of a research project, with the first version being simpler and more scaffolded, the second version being more complex, and the third version being advanced and challenging. This allows gifted and talented learners to work on more challenging assignments that are appropriate for their level of ability.

Flexible Grouping

Flexible grouping is a strategy that involves grouping students based on their ability levels and interests. This allows gifted and talented learners to work with other students who are at a similar level of ability and who share similar interests. This can help to increase motivation and engagement, as well as provide opportunities for peer learning and collaboration.

Independent Study Projects

Independent study projects are another way to differentiate instruction for gifted and talented learners. These projects allow learners to explore topics that are of interest to them in greater depth and detail. The teacher can provide resources and guidance to support the learner's independent research and learning, and can also provide opportunities for the learner to share their work with others.

Enrichment Activities

Enrichment activities are activities that provide gifted and talented learners with opportunities to explore topics in greater depth and detail. These activities can include field trips, guest speakers, simulations, and other hands-on experiences that allow learners to apply their knowledge in meaningful ways. Enrichment activities can be designed to meet the needs of individual learners or can be provided to the entire class.

Mentorship Programs

Mentorship programs are another way to differentiate instruction for gifted and talented learners. These programs pair students with mentors who are experts in their field of interest. The mentor can provide guidance, support, and feedback to the learner as they pursue their interests and goals. This can help to increase motivation, engagement, and self-efficacy.

Advanced Placement and Honors Courses

Advanced placement and honors courses are designed to challenge and engage gifted and talented learners. These courses provide learners with opportunities to study subjects in greater depth and detail and to earn college credit while still in high school. These courses are often more rigorous and challenging than regular courses and can provide learners with opportunities to develop their critical thinking, problem-solving, and research skills.

Competitions and Challenges

Competitions and challenges can be another way to differentiate instruction for gifted and talented learners. These competitions can be academic, artistic, or creative in nature and can provide learners with opportunities to showcase their talents and abilities. Competitions and challenges can be designed to meet the needs of individual learners or can be provided to the entire class.

Gifted and talented learners need differentiated instruction to challenge and engage them in meaningful ways. Teachers can use a variety of strategies, including curriculum compacting, tiered assignments, flexible grouping, independent study projects, enrichment activities, mentorship programs, advanced placement and honors courses, and competitions and challenges, to meet

Adapting instruction to different levels of giftedness

Adapting instruction to different levels of giftedness is a critical task for educators who work with gifted and talented students. Giftedness is not a one-dimensional construct; rather, it encompasses a range of abilities, interests, and characteristics. Thus, teachers must employ a variety of strategies to meet the diverse needs of gifted students. This article will explore some of these strategies and provide examples of how teachers can adapt instruction to different levels of giftedness.

Curriculum Compacting: This strategy involves streamlining the curriculum for gifted students by eliminating content that they have already mastered. The teacher can identify topics that students have already learned and allow them to focus on more advanced topics or to work on independent projects related to the subject matter.

Tiered Assignments: Tiered assignments are tasks that have different levels of complexity or depth. The teacher can offer several options for an assignment, each with different levels of challenge. For example, a writing assignment could include a basic level, a more challenging level, and an advanced level.

Independent Projects: Gifted students often thrive when given the opportunity to work on projects that reflect their interests and strengths. Teachers can encourage students to develop independent projects that align with the curriculum but also allow them to explore topics in greater depth or from different perspectives.

Flexible Grouping: Flexible grouping allows students to work with peers who share similar interests and abilities. Teachers can create small groups or learning communities based on students' strengths and interests, allowing them to work together on projects or activities that challenge them.

Acceleration: Acceleration involves allowing gifted students to move through the curriculum at a faster pace. This can take many forms, such as skipping a grade, taking advanced courses, or participating in enrichment activities outside of school.

Mentorship: Gifted students benefit from working with mentors who can provide guidance and support. Teachers can help identify mentors in the community who have expertise in a particular area of interest or who can offer advice on pursuing advanced educational opportunities.

Technology Integration: Technology can be a powerful tool for differentiating instruction for gifted students. Teachers can use online resources to offer additional challenge and enrichment opportunities or to provide access to advanced content that is not available in traditional classroom materials.

Socratic Seminars: Socratic seminars are structured discussions in which students examine complex questions and ideas. These seminars provide an opportunity for gifted students to engage with challenging topics in a supportive environment that encourages critical thinking and debate.

Self-Directed Learning: Gifted students often enjoy taking ownership of their learning and pursuing topics that interest them outside of the classroom. Teachers can provide guidance and support to help students identify and pursue their own learning goals.

Differentiated Feedback: Gifted students benefit from specific and detailed feedback on their work. Teachers can provide differentiated feedback that recognizes the strengths of the student's work and offers suggestions for improvement that are appropriate for their level of ability.

Adapting instruction to different levels of giftedness requires creativity, flexibility, and a deep understanding of students' strengths and needs. By employing a variety of strategies, teachers can provide gifted students with opportunities to learn, grow, and thrive.

Addressing the social and emotional needs of gifted and talented learners

Gifted and talented learners often have unique social and emotional needs that must be addressed in the classroom. These students may struggle with feelings of isolation, boredom, and frustration when their academic needs are not met. Additionally, they may face social and emotional challenges related to their exceptional abilities, such as difficulty fitting in with peers or pressure to constantly excel.

To support the social and emotional needs of gifted and talented learners, teachers can implement a variety of strategies. These include:

Building a positive classroom culture: A positive and inclusive classroom culture can help gifted and talented learners feel valued and connected. Teachers can promote a positive classroom culture by establishing clear expectations for behavior, encouraging collaboration and teamwork, and providing opportunities for all students to participate in classroom discussions and activities.

Providing opportunities for peer interaction: Gifted and talented learners may feel isolated if they are the only ones in the classroom with exceptional abilities. Teachers can provide opportunities for these students to interact with their peers, such as through small group work or collaborative projects.

Offering challenge and complexity: Gifted and talented learners need academic challenges that go beyond the standard curriculum. Teachers can provide these challenges by offering extension activities, independent research projects, or advanced coursework. Additionally, teachers can provide complexity by encouraging students to think critically and engage in higher-level thinking.

Encouraging self-reflection and self-regulation: Gifted and talented learners may struggle with perfectionism or feelings of inadequacy. Teachers can help these students develop self-reflection and self-regulation skills by encouraging them to reflect on their learning process, set realistic goals, and recognize their own strengths and weaknesses.

Providing support for social and emotional needs: Gifted and talented learners may need support from teachers or school counselors to address social and emotional challenges related to their exceptional abilities. Teachers can provide this support by offering counseling or mentoring services, facilitating peer support groups, or connecting students with outside resources.

Encouraging healthy work-life balance: Gifted and talented learners may feel pressure to constantly excel academically, which can lead to burnout and stress. Teachers can encourage

127

these students to maintain a healthy work-life balance by providing opportunities for physical activity, social interaction, and relaxation.

In addition to these strategies, it is important for teachers to communicate with gifted and talented learners and their families to ensure that their social and emotional needs are being met. Teachers should also work with other school professionals, such as counselors or administrators, to ensure that gifted and talented learners are receiving the support they need to thrive academically and emotionally. By addressing the social and emotional needs of gifted and talented learners, teachers can help these students reach their full potential and develop into confident, well-rounded individuals.

CHAPTER 11

DIFFERENTIATING INSTRUCTION FOR STUDENTS WITH DISABILITIES

Every child has the right to receive an education, and this includes students with disabilities. These students face unique challenges in the classroom and require specialized support to reach their full potential. As a teacher, it is essential to understand the needs of students with disabilities to provide them with the best possible education. In this article, we will discuss the different types of disabilities, the impact of disabilities on learning, and strategies for supporting students with disabilities.

Types of disabilities

There are many types of disabilities that can affect students, and each one requires different strategies and accommodations to ensure that the student can succeed in the classroom. Some of the most common types of disabilities include:

Intellectual disabilities: These are disabilities that affect a student's cognitive functioning, including their ability to learn, reason, and problem-solve.

Learning disabilities: These are disabilities that affect a student's ability to process information, including reading, writing, and math.

Autism spectrum disorders: These are disabilities that affect a student's ability to communicate, socialize, and interact with others.

Attention deficit hyperactivity disorder (ADHD): This is a disability that affects a student's ability to focus, pay attention, and control their impulses.

Emotional and behavioral disorders: These are disabilities that affect a student's emotional and behavioral functioning, including their ability to regulate their emotions and behavior.

Impact of disabilities on learning:

Students with disabilities face unique challenges in the classroom that can impact their learning. These challenges can include difficulty processing information, trouble with communication and socialization, and emotional and behavioral challenges. As a result, students with disabilities may require different types of support and accommodations to help them succeed in the classroom.

Strategies for supporting students with disabilities

As a teacher, it is essential to provide students with disabilities with the support and accommodations they need to succeed in the classroom. Here are some strategies for supporting students with disabilities:

Create an inclusive classroom environment: This means creating a classroom culture where all students feel valued and included, regardless of their abilities. This can be done by using inclusive language, celebrating diversity, and promoting acceptance and understanding.

Use differentiated instruction: This means tailoring your teaching methods to meet the unique needs of each student. This can involve using a variety of teaching strategies, such as visual aids, manipulatives, and technology, to help students with different learning styles.

Provide accommodations and modifications: Accommodations are changes made to the classroom environment or teaching methods to help students with disabilities learn. Modifications are changes made to the curriculum itself. Examples of accommodations and modifications include extra time on assignments, assistive technology, and simplified language.

Use assistive technology: Assistive technology can help students with disabilities access the curriculum and participate in classroom activities. Examples of assistive technology include text-to-speech software, speech recognition software, and alternative input devices.

Work with parents and other professionals: It is important to work with parents and other professionals, such as special education teachers and speech therapists, to ensure that students with disabilities receive the support they need both inside and outside the classroom.

Provide emotional and behavioral support: Students with disabilities may face emotional and behavioral challenges that can impact their learning. Providing emotional and behavioral support can include things like positive reinforcement, behavior contracts, and counseling.

Use Universal Design for Learning (UDL): UDL is an approach to teaching that provides multiple means of representation, expression, and engagement to meet the needs of all learners, including those with disabilities.

Strategies for differentiating instruction for students with disabilities

Differentiating instruction for students with disabilities is essential to provide them with equal opportunities for learning and academic success. It involves the use of various instructional strategies and modifications to meet the specific needs of individual students with disabilities. Here are some effective strategies for differentiating instruction for students with disabilities:

Provide Accessible Instructional Materials: Providing accessible instructional materials is one of the essential strategies for differentiating instruction for students with disabilities. Teachers can modify materials by using enlarged print, braille, audio materials, or other assistive technologies. This will help students with visual impairments, hearing impairments, and other disabilities to access the content.

Use Multisensory Instruction: Using multisensory instruction can be an effective way to differentiate instruction for students with disabilities. This approach engages multiple senses, such as touch, sight, and hearing, to help students process information. For example, teachers can use hands-on activities or manipulatives to help students with learning disabilities understand math concepts.

Provide Individualized Instruction: Individualized instruction is an effective strategy for differentiating instruction for students with disabilities. Teachers can provide one-on-one instruction, small group instruction, or pull-out instruction to meet the specific needs of individual students. This approach can help students with disabilities learn at their own pace and receive the support they need to succeed.

Use Assistive Technology: Assistive technology can be an effective way to differentiate instruction for students with disabilities. There are various types of assistive technology available, such as text-to-speech software, speech-to-text software, and adaptive keyboards. These tools can help students with disabilities access and engage with the content and perform academic tasks more effectively.

Scaffold Instruction: Scaffolding instruction is an effective way to differentiate instruction for students with disabilities. Teachers can break down complex tasks into smaller, more manageable steps, and provide support as needed. This approach can help students with disabilities build confidence and develop new skills.

Incorporate Universal Design for Learning (UDL): UDL is a framework that promotes inclusive instruction for all students, including those with disabilities. UDL involves providing multiple means of representation, expression, and engagement to help all students access and engage with the content. Teachers can use UDL principles to differentiate instruction for students with disabilities by providing various options for learning and expression.

Provide Clear and Consistent Expectations: Providing clear and consistent expectations is an essential strategy for differentiating instruction for students with disabilities. Teachers can use visual aids, such as charts and graphs, to help students understand expectations and track progress. Consistent routines and expectations can help students with disabilities feel more confident and comfortable in the learning environment.

Use Positive Reinforcement: Positive reinforcement is an effective strategy for motivating and encouraging students with disabilities. Teachers can use verbal praise, tokens, or other incentives to reward positive behavior and academic progress. This approach can help students with disabilities feel more engaged and motivated to learn.

Collaborate with Specialists: Collaborating with specialists, such as special education teachers, occupational therapists, and speech therapists, can be an effective way to differentiate instruction for students with disabilities. These specialists can provide valuable insights and recommendations for adapting instruction and meeting the specific needs of individual students.

Build a Positive and Supportive Learning Environment: Building a positive and supportive learning environment is an essential strategy for differentiating instruction for students with disabilities. Teachers can create a welcoming and inclusive learning environment that promotes student engagement and fosters a sense of community. This approach can help students with disabilities feel valued and supported in the learning environment.

Adapting instruction to different types of disabilities

When it comes to adapting instruction for students with disabilities, it's important to keep in mind that different disabilities will require different approaches. Here are some strategies for adapting instruction to meet the needs of students with different types of disabilities:

Physical disabilities: Students with physical disabilities may have difficulty participating in activities that require mobility. In order to adapt instruction for these students, teachers may need to provide alternative activities or make modifications to existing activities to accommodate the student's needs. For example, a student who uses a wheelchair may need a modified seating arrangement in order to participate in a science experiment or a different type of manipulative that can be used without fine motor skills.

Visual impairments: Students with visual impairments may need accommodations such as large print materials or audio versions of text. Teachers can also provide tactile learning experiences, such as raised maps or 3D models, to help these students better understand concepts.

Hearing impairments: Students with hearing impairments may require a variety of accommodations depending on the severity of their impairment. Teachers can use visual aids such as videos with subtitles or sign language interpreters. Additionally, seating arrangements can be adjusted to allow the student to see the teacher's face and mouth during instruction.

Learning disabilities: Students with learning disabilities may struggle with reading, writing, or math skills. To adapt instruction for these students, teachers can provide alternative methods of presenting information such as videos, audio recordings, or graphic organizers. Additionally, teachers can provide extra practice opportunities and offer personalized feedback to help students master the skills they need.

Autism spectrum disorder: Students with autism may benefit from visual aids, such as picture schedules, and may need extra support to stay on task and regulate their emotions. Teachers can also provide clear and concise instructions and avoid sensory overload by minimizing distractions in the classroom.

When adapting instruction for students with disabilities, it's important to consider the unique needs of each individual student and to collaborate with support staff such as special education teachers and paraprofessionals. By working together and using a variety of strategies, teachers can ensure that students with disabilities have access to the same curriculum as their peers and are able to succeed academically.

Addressing the social and emotional needs of students with disabilities

Students with disabilities often face social and emotional challenges in addition to their academic struggles. As a result, it is important for teachers to provide support and create an inclusive classroom environment that meets the unique needs of these students. In this article, we will discuss some strategies for addressing the social and emotional needs of students with disabilities.

Foster a positive classroom environment

Creating a positive classroom environment is essential for all students, but it is especially important for those with disabilities. Teachers can create a positive classroom environment by establishing clear expectations for behavior, providing positive feedback, and celebrating successes. Teachers can also create a sense of community within the classroom by encouraging students to work together, promoting a sense of belonging, and providing opportunities for students to participate in classroom decision-making.

Provide social skills instruction

Many students with disabilities struggle with social skills, which can lead to feelings of isolation and frustration. Providing social skills instruction can help these students learn how to interact with others and build positive relationships. Teachers can provide social skills instruction through direct teaching, modeling appropriate behaviors, and providing opportunities for practice and feedback.

Use assistive technology

Assistive technology can be a powerful tool for addressing the social and emotional needs of students with disabilities. For example, some students may benefit from using communication devices to express their thoughts and feelings, while others may benefit from using assistive technology to manage their emotions. Teachers can work with specialists to identify and implement appropriate assistive technology for their students.

Incorporate movement breaks

Students with disabilities may struggle with sitting still for long periods of time, which can lead to increased frustration and anxiety. Incorporating movement breaks into the school day can help these students release energy and refocus their attention. Teachers can provide movement breaks by leading physical activities or providing opportunities for students to move around the classroom.

Address bullying and teasing

Students with disabilities are often targets for bullying and teasing, which can have a negative impact on their social and emotional well-being. Teachers can address bullying and teasing by establishing clear rules against this behavior, educating students about the negative impact of bullying, and providing opportunities for students to practice kindness and empathy.

Provide counseling services

Counseling services can be an important resource for students with disabilities who are struggling with social and emotional issues. Teachers can work with school counselors and other professionals to identify students who may benefit from counseling services and make appropriate referrals. Counseling services can provide students with a safe space to express their feelings and work through their challenges.

Involve parents and caregivers

Parents and caregivers play an important role in supporting the social and emotional needs of students with disabilities. Teachers can involve parents and caregivers by providing regular updates on their child's progress, communicating about any challenges or concerns, and working collaboratively to create a plan for supporting the student's social and emotional well-being.

Supporting the social and emotional needs of students with disabilities is essential for creating an inclusive and supportive classroom environment. By fostering a positive classroom environment, providing social skills instruction, using assistive technology, incorporating movement breaks, addressing bullying and teasing, providing counseling services, and involving parents and caregivers, teachers can help students with disabilities thrive both academically and socially.

CHAPTER 12

TECHNOLOGY TO SUPPORT DIFFERENTIATED INSTRUCTION

Differentiated instruction is a teaching approach that recognizes that students learn in different ways and at different paces, and that teachers should adjust their instruction to meet the needs of individual learners. Technology can be a powerful tool for differentiating instruction, as it provides teachers with new ways to deliver content, assess student learning, and personalize instruction.

In this unit, we will explore the role of technology in differentiated instruction, and provide some examples of how teachers can use technology to support differentiated instruction in their classrooms.

Delivering Content

One of the most important ways that technology can support differentiated instruction is by providing teachers with new ways to deliver content to students. For example, teachers can use multimedia resources, such as videos, podcasts, and interactive simulations, to present information in a variety of formats that appeal to different learning styles.

Students who are visual learners may benefit from watching videos that illustrate key concepts, while auditory learners may prefer to listen to podcasts or lectures. Interactive simulations can be particularly effective for kinesthetic learners, as they allow students to manipulate virtual objects and experiment with different scenarios.

Online resources can also be used to provide students with access to a wider range of reading materials. For example, teachers can use e-books and online libraries to provide students with access to books and articles that are tailored to their interests and reading levels. This can be particularly useful for students who struggle with reading or who have difficulty accessing traditional print materials.

Assessing Learning

Another important role that technology can play in differentiated instruction is in assessing student learning. Traditional forms of assessment, such as written tests and quizzes, may not be effective for all learners, particularly those who have difficulty with written expression or who require accommodations to access written materials.

Technology can be used to provide alternative forms of assessment that allow students to demonstrate their understanding in different ways. For example, teachers can use online quizzes, surveys, and polls to assess student learning, as well as online discussion forums, which allow students to engage in collaborative learning activities and demonstrate their understanding of key concepts.

Digital portfolios can also be used to document student learning and growth over time, providing a more comprehensive view of student progress than traditional assessment methods.

Personalizing Instruction

Finally, technology can be used to personalize instruction for individual learners. Personalized learning is an approach that focuses on providing each student with the resources and support they need to achieve their learning goals.

Technology can be used to provide students with personalized learning experiences that are tailored to their interests, learning styles, and abilities. For example, teachers can use learning management systems (LMS) to create custom learning pathways that guide students through the curriculum at their own pace.

Adaptive learning technologies can also be used to provide students with personalized learning experiences. These technologies use machine learning algorithms to analyze student data and adjust the learning experience to meet the needs of each individual learner. For example, an adaptive learning platform may provide students with targeted feedback, adjust the difficulty level of assignments, or provide additional resources to support struggling learners.

Technology has the potential to be a powerful tool for differentiating instruction, providing teachers with new ways to deliver content, assess student learning, and personalize instruction. However, it is important to remember that technology is not a substitute for effective teaching practices, and that teachers must still use their professional judgment to determine the most effective strategies for meeting the needs of individual learners.

Teachers should also be mindful of the potential limitations of technology, particularly in the context of equity and access. Not all students have equal access to technology and resources, and teachers must be proactive in ensuring that all students have

141

equal opportunities to learn and succeed. With these considerations in mind, technology can be an effective tool for supporting differentiated instruction and improving student learning outcomes.

Differentiated instruction tools and resources

Differentiated instruction (DI) is a teaching approach that recognizes the diversity of students' learning styles, abilities, and backgrounds. This approach involves providing multiple ways for students to learn and demonstrating an understanding of students' individual needs by adapting instruction, assessment, and classroom environment to optimize learning. Technology has become an increasingly important tool in supporting differentiated instruction in today's classrooms. In this article, we will discuss some of the most effective tools and resources for implementing differentiated instruction with the help of technology.

Learning Management Systems (LMS)

A Learning Management System (LMS) is an online platform that allows educators to create, manage, and deliver content and assessments to students. An LMS can be used to differentiate instruction by allowing teachers to create different paths for students to follow based on their learning needs. For example, a teacher can create a set of resources or activities for students who need extra support in a particular area, while providing more challenging work for advanced learners. Popular LMS options include Google Classroom, Schoology, Canvas, and Edmodo.

Adaptive Learning Software

Adaptive learning software is designed to adapt to students' learning needs and provide personalized instruction based on their progress. These programs use algorithms and artificial intelligence to identify each student's strengths and weaknesses and adjust the difficulty level of content accordingly. Some popular adaptive learning software options include DreamBox, IXL, and Khan Academy.

Video-based Learning

Video-based learning is a highly effective way to differentiate instruction. Teachers can use videos to introduce new concepts, reinforce skills, or provide additional support to students who need it. Video resources such as TED-Ed, Discovery Education, and YouTube are excellent tools for teachers to find high-quality educational videos that can be used for differentiated instruction.

Podcasts and Audio Books

Podcasts and audio books are powerful tools for differentiating instruction in the classroom. Students can listen to podcasts or audio books that align with their interests, learning styles, or reading level. Teachers can use these resources to provide students with access to engaging content and to develop listening and comprehension skills. Some popular podcast and audio book resources for education include Storynory, Audible, and Spotify.

Gamification

Gamification is a teaching strategy that uses game-like elements to motivate and engage students. Teachers can use gamification to differentiate instruction by providing students with different levels of challenges or rewards based on their learning needs.

Popular gamification resources for education include Classcraft, Kahoot!, and Quizlet.

Digital Whiteboards and Mind Mapping Tools

Digital whiteboards and mind mapping tools can be used to differentiate instruction by allowing students to visualize and organize information in a way that works best for them. Teachers can use these tools to create collaborative activities and interactive lessons that allow students to work together and develop critical thinking skills. Some popular digital whiteboard and mind mapping tools include Padlet, Miro, and Google Jamboard.

Assistive Technology

Assistive technology refers to devices and tools that help students with disabilities overcome challenges and participate in learning. These tools can be used to differentiate instruction by providing students with individualized support, such as text-to-speech, speech-to-text, or digital tools that help with organization and note-taking. Some popular assistive technology resources for education include Read&Write, Co:Writer, and Notability.

Using technology to support student engagement and motivation

Technology has become an integral part of our daily lives, and it has also revolutionized the way we teach and learn. In today's classrooms, technology is being used to support differentiated instruction by promoting student engagement and motivation. Technology tools and resources can provide multiple ways for students to access and interact with content, which can help to increase their interest and investment in learning.

Here are some examples of how technology can be used to support student engagement and motivation in differentiated instruction:

Interactive Whiteboards: Interactive whiteboards are large displays that can be used to project and manipulate digital content. These boards can help teachers to present information in an engaging way by allowing them to incorporate multimedia elements such as videos, images, and audio. They also provide opportunities for students to interact with the content by using touch, digital pens, or other input devices.

Gamification: Gamification involves incorporating game-like elements into the learning process to increase student motivation and engagement. Teachers can use a variety of digital games and simulations to help students learn, practice, and apply new concepts in a fun and interactive way. For example, teachers can use educational games like Kahoot or Quizizz to gamify assessments and reinforce learning objectives.

Learning Management Systems: Learning management systems (LMS) are web-based platforms that allow teachers to manage and deliver online content and activities. LMS can provide students with personalized learning experiences that are tailored to their individual needs and interests. Teachers can use LMS to create and share content, provide feedback, and track student progress.

Digital Storytelling: Digital storytelling involves using digital tools and multimedia to tell stories. It can be used to enhance student engagement and motivation by providing a creative outlet for students to express themselves and demonstrate their understanding of concepts. For example, students can create videos, podcasts, or animations to showcase their learning.

Virtual and Augmented Reality: Virtual and augmented reality are technologies that can create immersive and interactive experiences for students. These technologies can be used to bring learning to life by providing students with opportunities to explore and interact with virtual environments. For example, students can use virtual reality headsets to explore historical landmarks, museums, or natural environments.

Personalized Learning Platforms: Personalized learning platforms are digital tools that can be used to deliver content and activities that are tailored to each student's individual needs and interests. These platforms use data and analytics to create customized learning pathways for students, which can help to increase their engagement and motivation.

Adaptive Learning Software: Adaptive learning software uses artificial intelligence and machine learning algorithms to adjust content and activities based on each student's performance and learning needs. These tools can provide students with personalized learning experiences that are designed to maximize their learning outcomes.

Addressing the digital divide

The digital divide refers to the gap between those who have access to technology and those who do not. This divide exists both globally and domestically, and it has a significant impact on students' academic success. According to the National Center for Education Statistics, students who lack access to technology at home are at a disadvantage compared to their peers who have access. These students are more likely to have lower grades, lower graduation rates, and fewer post-secondary education opportunities.

To address the digital divide, schools and districts have implemented various strategies to provide students with access to technology. One approach is to provide students with devices, such as laptops or tablets, for use both in and out of school. Another approach is to provide internet access to students' homes through hotspots or partnerships with internet service providers. Additionally, some schools have created technology labs or computer centers for students to use during and after school.

While these strategies are essential, they may not be enough to address the digital divide fully. Students may still lack the necessary skills to effectively use technology for learning, such as online research, digital communication, and multimedia production. Therefore, it is essential to provide training and support to both students and teachers to ensure that technology is used effectively and meaningfully.

One way to address the digital divide is to provide students with digital literacy training. Digital literacy encompasses a range of skills, including basic computer skills, internet navigation, and the ability to evaluate online information critically. By providing students with digital literacy training, they can become more confident and competent users of technology, which can translate to better academic performance and success in the workplace.

Another way to address the digital divide is to provide teachers with professional development opportunities focused on integrating technology into their instruction. Professional development can help teachers develop the necessary skills and strategies to effectively use technology for differentiated instruction, such as using digital tools to provide students with individualized feedback, creating online resources and activities to engage students, and using technology to facilitate communication and collaboration among students.

In addition to providing training and support, schools can also leverage existing technology tools and resources to address the digital divide. For example, digital textbooks and online resources can provide access to educational content that may be unavailable in traditional print formats. Additionally, digital tools such as adaptive software and virtual manipulatives can provide students with individualized and interactive learning experiences that cater to their unique needs and preferences.

To ensure equitable access to technology, schools can also consider partnering with community organizations or businesses to provide additional resources and support. For example, local libraries may have computer labs or provide internet access to community members, and businesses may donate or provide discounted devices to schools.

Addressing the digital divide is essential to ensure equitable access to education and opportunities for academic success. Schools and districts can take various approaches, including providing students with devices and internet access, offering digital literacy training to both students and teachers, and leveraging existing technology tools and resources to support differentiated instruction. By taking these steps, schools can help close the digital divide and ensure that all students have access to the technology and resources necessary to succeed in school and beyond.

CHAPTER 13

COLLABORATION AND
DIFFERENTIATED INSTRUCTION

Collaboration is a crucial component of differentiated instruction. It involves working together with other educators, professionals, and stakeholders to develop, implement, and evaluate differentiated instruction. Collaboration promotes the exchange of ideas, knowledge, and experiences, and it helps teachers to better understand and address the diverse needs of their students.

Collaboration can take many forms, such as co-planning, co-teaching, team teaching, professional learning communities, and interdisciplinary teams. These forms of collaboration enable teachers to share their expertise, resources, and strategies for differentiating instruction. They also foster a culture of continuous learning and improvement, where teachers can learn from each other and develop new skills and knowledge.

Co-planning is a common form of collaboration in differentiated instruction. It involves teachers working together to design and develop differentiated lessons and activities that meet the diverse needs of their students. Co-planning allows teachers to share their knowledge of the subject matter and their understanding of their students' strengths and weaknesses. By working together, teachers can develop strategies that will engage and challenge all learners, including those with disabilities, English language learners, and gifted and talented students.

Co-teaching is another form of collaboration in differentiated instruction. It involves two or more teachers working together in the same classroom to provide differentiated instruction to students. This approach allows teachers to differentiate instruction more effectively by providing targeted support and interventions to students who need it. Co-teaching also promotes collaboration, as teachers can share their experiences and knowledge of effective instructional strategies.

Professional learning communities (PLCs) are collaborative groups of educators who share a common goal of improving student learning. PLCs provide a forum for teachers to collaborate, share ideas, and discuss best practices in differentiated instruction. They also provide a platform for teachers to engage in ongoing professional development and learning.

Interdisciplinary teams are another form of collaboration in differentiated instruction. They involve teachers from different subject areas working together to develop and implement differentiated instruction across multiple subjects. Interdisciplinary teams can provide a more comprehensive and integrated approach to differentiated instruction, as teachers can leverage their expertise in different subject areas to develop more effective instruction.

In addition to collaboration among teachers, differentiated instruction also requires collaboration with parents, families, and other stakeholders. Parents and families play a critical role in supporting and reinforcing differentiated instruction outside of the classroom. Teachers can collaborate with parents and families by providing resources and strategies that they can use at home to support their child's learning. They can also involve parents and families in the development of individualized learning plans and progress monitoring.

Collaboration is a critical component of differentiated instruction. It enables teachers to better understand and address the diverse needs of their students, and it fosters a culture of continuous learning and improvement. Differentiated instruction requires collaboration among teachers, as well as collaboration with parents, families, and other stakeholders. Through collaboration, teachers can develop and implement more effective and impactful instruction that meets the needs of all learners.

Collaboration strategies for teachers, parents, and specialists

Collaboration is a vital aspect of differentiated instruction. It involves working together to ensure that all students receive high-quality instruction that is tailored to their individual needs. Collaboration helps teachers to share their knowledge, expertise, and experience to provide students with a holistic and comprehensive learning experience. Effective collaboration among teachers, parents, and specialists can improve student outcomes and support the success of differentiated instruction.

Here are some collaboration strategies that teachers, parents, and specialists can use to support differentiated instruction:

Regular communication: Teachers, parents, and specialists should establish regular communication channels to discuss students' needs and progress. Teachers can share updates on students' academic performance, and specialists can provide information on any additional support that students may require. Parents can share information on students' strengths, weaknesses,

151

and interests. Regular communication can help to ensure that all parties are aware of students' needs and are working together to address them.

Co-planning: Teachers can work collaboratively to plan instruction that meets the needs of all students in their classes. Co-planning involves working together to identify learning objectives, assessment strategies, and instructional materials that are appropriate for each student's needs. Co-planning can help to ensure that instruction is differentiated and that all students receive high-quality instruction.

Co-teaching: Co-teaching involves two or more teachers working together in the classroom to provide instruction to students. Co-teaching can be used to support differentiated instruction by allowing teachers to provide targeted instruction to small groups of students. For example, one teacher could work with a group of students who need additional support while another teacher works with a group of students who are ready for more advanced instruction.

Parent-teacher conferences: Parent-teacher conferences provide an opportunity for parents and teachers to discuss students' progress and needs. These conferences can be used to share information on students' strengths, weaknesses, and interests, and to develop strategies to support their learning. Parent-teacher conferences can help to ensure that parents are aware of their child's progress and are working collaboratively with teachers to support their child's learning.

Professional development: Teachers, parents, and specialists should engage in ongoing professional development to enhance their knowledge and skills. Professional development can provide teachers with the tools and strategies they need to effectively differentiate instruction. It can also help parents and specialists to better understand the needs of students and how they can support their learning.

Multi-disciplinary teams: Multi-disciplinary teams involve a group of professionals from different disciplines who work together to support students' learning. These teams can include teachers, specialists, counselors, and administrators. Multi-disciplinary teams can provide a comprehensive approach to addressing students' needs and can ensure that all aspects of their learning are addressed.

Data analysis: Collaboration can be enhanced by analyzing data on students' performance. This can involve reviewing assessment results, attendance records, and other data sources to identify patterns and trends in students' learning. Data analysis can help teachers, parents, and specialists to identify areas where students need additional support and to develop strategies to address these needs.

Collaboration is an essential component of differentiated instruction. Teachers, parents, and specialists should work together to ensure that all students receive high-quality instruction that is tailored to their individual needs. Collaboration strategies, such as regular communication, co-planning, co-teaching, and parent-teacher conferences, can support differentiated instruction and improve student outcomes. Additionally, ongoing professional development, multi-disciplinary teams, and data analysis can help to enhance collaboration and ensure that all aspects of students' learning are addressed.

Building a team approach to differentiated instruction

Differentiated instruction is a teaching approach that recognizes that students have unique learning styles, interests, and abilities, and therefore require different methods of instruction and support to succeed academically. Creating a successful differentiated instruction program requires collaboration among various stakeholders, including teachers, parents, and specialists. A team approach to differentiated instruction can enhance student learning and success by combining the expertise and resources of various stakeholders.

Collaboration among teachers is a crucial component of differentiated instruction. Teachers can work together to plan and implement instruction that meets the needs of all students. Collaborative planning can help teachers identify students who require additional support, determine the best teaching strategies to meet their needs, and monitor student progress. Collaborative planning can also help ensure that all students are receiving the same learning opportunities regardless of the teacher they have.

Parents also play an important role in supporting differentiated instruction. Teachers can communicate with parents about their child's learning style, interests, and strengths and involve them in the development of their child's learning plan. Parents can provide information about their child's learning outside of the classroom and can also support learning at home. Teachers can also provide parents with resources and strategies to support their child's learning.

Specialists, such as speech and language therapists, reading specialists, and special education teachers, can provide additional support to teachers and students. Specialists can work with teachers to identify students who require additional support and provide resources and strategies to meet their needs. They can also work with students individually or in small groups to provide additional instruction and support.

A team approach to differentiated instruction can also help address issues of student motivation and engagement. Teachers can work together to identify strategies that motivate and engage students with diverse learning needs. They can also develop resources, such as games, interactive activities, and technology-based learning tools, that appeal to different learning styles and interests.

Creating a team approach to differentiated instruction requires effective communication and collaboration among stakeholders. Teachers can establish regular meetings to discuss student progress, share ideas and resources, and plan instruction collaboratively. They can also use technology to facilitate communication and collaboration, such as video conferencing, shared online documents, and online discussion forums.

In addition to regular communication and collaboration, it is important to establish clear roles and responsibilities for each stakeholder. Teachers can ensure that parents and specialists are informed about the instructional strategies being used and the progress of their child or student. They can also involve parents and specialists in the development of the student's learning plan and provide them with resources and strategies to support learning at home.

A team approach to differentiated instruction can help ensure that all students have access to high-quality instruction and support. Collaboration among teachers, parents, and specialists can enhance student learning and success by combining the expertise and resources of various stakeholders. Effective communication and collaboration, clear roles and responsibilities, and a focus on student motivation and engagement are essential components of a successful team approach to differentiated instruction.

Addressing communication barriers in collaboration

Collaboration among teachers, parents, and specialists is essential in implementing effective differentiated instruction. However, communication barriers can hinder the collaboration process, resulting in misunderstandings, lack of trust, and failure to achieve the desired outcomes. Communication barriers are factors that interfere with the effectiveness of communication between individuals or groups. These barriers can take many forms, such as language differences, cultural differences, technological barriers, and different expectations and goals.

Effective communication in a collaborative team requires that all parties understand and respect each other's needs and goals. Here are some strategies to help address communication barriers and build effective collaboration in differentiated instruction:

Establish clear communication channels

The first step in addressing communication barriers is to establish clear communication channels. Each member of the team should know who to communicate with and how to reach them. This may involve setting up regular meetings, using email, video conferencing, or phone calls. Communication channels should be accessible to all team members, including those with disabilities, and should take into account language and cultural differences.

Develop a shared language and vocabulary

Effective communication in a collaborative team requires a shared language and vocabulary. Teachers, parents, and specialists may use different terms and jargon to describe the same concepts, leading to misunderstandings. To overcome this barrier, the team should develop a shared language and vocabulary to ensure that everyone understands the terminology used. The team should also avoid using technical terms and jargon that may be unfamiliar to some team members.

Establish trust and respect

Building trust and respect among team members is essential for effective communication. Each member of the team should value the knowledge and expertise of others and recognize the contributions they make. This can be achieved through active listening, acknowledging each other's contributions, and providing feedback. The team should also be open and honest about their goals, concerns, and challenges.

Understand cultural differences

Cultural differences can be a significant communication barrier in collaborative teams. Team members should take the time to understand and appreciate the different cultural perspectives and practices of others. This can be achieved by learning about each other's cultures, customs, and values. It is also essential to avoid making assumptions based on cultural stereotypes or biases.

Address language barriers

Language barriers can be a significant challenge in collaborative teams, especially when working with families or specialists who speak a different language. The team should use translation services, interpreters, or other tools to ensure that everyone understands the information being shared. When working with families, it is also important to use plain language and avoid technical jargon.

Use technology to enhance communication

Technology can be an effective tool for enhancing communication in a collaborative team. Video conferencing, instant messaging, and other digital tools can help team members communicate in real-time, regardless of their location. These tools can also be used to share documents, videos, and other resources that support the differentiated instruction process.

Develop a shared vision and goals

Collaboration requires a shared vision and goals. The team should work together to develop a shared understanding of what they hope to achieve and how they plan to do it. The team should also establish clear goals and objectives that are measurable and achievable. This can help to ensure that all team members are working towards a common goal and can help to overcome communication barriers that may arise.

Communication barriers can be a significant challenge in collaborative teams, but they can be overcome through effective communication strategies. By establishing clear communication channels, developing a shared language and vocabulary, building trust and respect, understanding cultural differences, addressing language barriers, using technology to enhance communication, and developing a shared vision and goals, collaborative teams can work together to support effective differentiated instruction.

CHAPTER 14

PROFESSIONAL DEVELOPMENT FOR DIFFERENTIATED INSTRUCTION

Professional development is critical in ensuring that educators have the necessary skills, knowledge, and resources to implement effective differentiated instruction strategies. Professional development provides opportunities for educators to learn about research-based best practices, explore new strategies, and reflect on their practice.

Effective professional development for differentiated instruction should be ongoing, collaborative, and aligned with the needs of educators and students. It should provide opportunities for teachers to learn from experts in the field, collaborate with colleagues, and receive feedback on their practice. Professional development should also incorporate technology and other innovative tools and resources that can support differentiated instruction.

The benefits of professional development for differentiated instruction are numerous. It can help teachers improve their instructional practices, increase student engagement and motivation, and improve student achievement. Professional development can also help teachers develop a deeper understanding of their students' diverse learning needs and abilities, and create more inclusive and responsive learning environments.

There are several types of professional development opportunities that can support differentiated instruction, including workshops, seminars, conferences, and online courses. These opportunities can be offered by schools, districts, universities, and professional organizations.

Workshops and seminars are often focused on a specific topic or strategy related to differentiated instruction. These opportunities may be led by experts in the field or by experienced educators who have successfully implemented differentiated instruction strategies in their classrooms. Workshops and seminars can be offered in-person or online, and may include hands-on activities, case studies, and opportunities for collaboration and reflection.

Conferences provide educators with an opportunity to learn about the latest research and best practices related to differentiated instruction. Conferences may include keynote speakers, panel discussions, and breakout sessions focused on a variety of topics related to differentiated instruction. Educators can attend conferences in-person or online, and can often earn professional development credits or certifications.

Online courses and webinars provide educators with a convenient and flexible way to learn about differentiated instruction strategies. These opportunities can be accessed from anywhere with an internet connection and can be completed at the teacher's own pace. Online courses and webinars can include videos, interactive activities, and opportunities for discussion and collaboration.

In addition to formal professional development opportunities, educators can also engage in informal professional development activities such as reading professional literature, participating in online communities of practice, and collaborating with colleagues.

It is important for schools and districts to provide educators with the time, resources, and support necessary to engage in professional development for differentiated instruction. This may include providing substitute teachers to cover classes, allocating funds for professional development activities, and providing access to technology and other resources.

Schools and districts can also support professional development for differentiated instruction by creating a culture of continuous learning and improvement. This can be achieved by encouraging collaboration among teachers, providing opportunities for feedback and reflection, and recognizing and celebrating successes.

Professional development is essential for educators to effectively implement differentiated instruction strategies. It provides opportunities for teachers to learn new skills, reflect on their practice, and improve student outcomes. Schools and districts should provide a variety of professional development opportunities and support a culture of continuous learning and improvement.

Differentiated instruction training and resources

Differentiated instruction is an effective instructional approach that helps teachers tailor their lessons to meet the diverse learning needs of their students. This approach requires teachers to be skilled in assessing their students' learning needs and then adapting their instruction accordingly. However, many teachers may not have the knowledge or skills necessary to implement differentiated instruction effectively. Professional development can provide the necessary training and resources to support teachers in this endeavor.

Professional development for differentiated instruction should focus on the following areas:

Understanding the principles of differentiated instruction: Teachers need to understand the underlying principles of differentiated instruction, including the importance of assessing student needs, providing flexible instruction, and incorporating a variety of instructional strategies.

Assessment strategies: Teachers need to know how to assess students' learning needs using a variety of assessment tools, including formative and summative assessments, pre-assessments, and self-assessments.

Instructional strategies: Teachers need to learn a variety of instructional strategies to support differentiated instruction, including flexible grouping, tiered assignments, choice boards, and learning menus.

Technology integration: Teachers need to know how to integrate technology into differentiated instruction, including the use of online learning platforms, educational apps, and digital resources.

Collaboration: Teachers need to understand the importance of collaboration in differentiated instruction and how to work effectively with other teachers, specialists, and parents to support student learning.

Professional development opportunities for differentiated instruction can take many forms, including:

Workshops and seminars: These can be offered by educational organizations, school districts, or individual schools. Workshops and seminars provide teachers with an opportunity to learn about differentiated instruction from experts in the field and to collaborate with other educators.

Online courses: Online courses provide teachers with the flexibility to learn about differentiated instruction at their own pace and on their own schedule. Online courses may include video lectures, readings, and interactive activities.

Conferences: Attending conferences focused on differentiated instruction provides teachers with an opportunity to learn from experts in the field and to network with other educators.

Professional learning communities (PLCs): PLCs are groups of teachers who work together to support student learning. PLCs can provide teachers with an opportunity to collaborate with others to develop and implement differentiated instruction strategies.

Coaching and mentoring: Coaching and mentoring can provide teachers with personalized support and guidance to help them develop and implement differentiated instruction strategies.

In addition to professional development opportunities, there are many resources available to support teachers in implementing differentiated instruction. These resources include:

Curriculum materials: Many curriculum materials include differentiated instruction strategies and resources. Teachers can use these resources to develop and implement differentiated instruction in their classrooms.

Educational apps and digital resources: There are many educational apps and digital resources available that can support differentiated instruction. These resources include online learning platforms, educational games, and digital resources that can be used to support student learning.

Assessment tools: There are many assessment tools available that can be used to assess student learning needs and progress. These tools include formative and summative assessments, pre-assessments, and self-assessments.

Collaboration tools: Collaboration tools, such as online discussion boards and video conferencing, can be used to support collaboration between teachers, specialists, and parents.

Professional organizations: Professional organizations, such as the National Association for Gifted Children, the Council for Exceptional Children, and the International Dyslexia Association, provide resources and support for teachers who work with diverse learners.

Professional development is essential to support teachers in implementing differentiated instruction effectively. Teachers need to have a strong understanding of the principles of differentiated instruction, assessment strategies, instructional strategies, technology integration, and collaboration. There are many professional development opportunities and resources available to support teachers in this endeavor, including workshops and seminars, online courses, conferences, professional learning communities,

Incorporating differentiated instruction into teacher evaluation and support

Incorporating differentiated instruction into teacher evaluation and support is an essential component of ensuring that all students receive the education they deserve. Differentiated instruction can be challenging for teachers to implement, especially if they have not received adequate training or support in this area. Therefore, it is essential to incorporate differentiated instruction into the teacher evaluation and support process to ensure that teachers have the necessary skills and resources to provide high-quality instruction to all students.

Teacher evaluation and support should be designed to encourage and support teachers in their efforts to differentiate instruction. This means that teachers should be provided with the necessary resources, training, and support to help them effectively differentiate instruction for all students. Additionally, teacher evaluations should take into account how well teachers are implementing differentiated instruction and supporting the needs of all students.

One approach to incorporating differentiated instruction into teacher evaluation and support is to use a rubric or framework that explicitly addresses differentiated instruction. Such a rubric would outline the various components of differentiated instruction and provide specific examples of how teachers can effectively implement differentiated instruction in their classrooms. The rubric could also include indicators of success that would help teachers assess their progress in implementing differentiated instruction effectively.

Another approach to incorporating differentiated instruction into teacher evaluation and support is to provide ongoing professional development opportunities. Professional development can take many forms, such as workshops, courses, and coaching sessions. It is essential to provide teachers with ongoing professional development opportunities that focus on differentiated instruction, as this will help them stay up to date with the latest research and best practices in this area.

Professional development opportunities should be tailored to meet the needs of individual teachers and should be designed to help them effectively implement differentiated instruction in their classrooms. It is also essential to provide teachers with access to resources and tools that will help them implement differentiated instruction effectively. This can include access to technology, online resources, and instructional materials.

Incorporating differentiated instruction into teacher evaluation and support is essential to ensure that all students receive high-quality instruction that meets their unique needs. It is important to provide teachers with the necessary resources, training, and support to help them effectively implement differentiated instruction in their classrooms. By doing so, we can ensure that all students have the opportunity to reach their full potential and succeed in school and beyond.

Addressing resistance to change in professional development

Resistance to change is a common issue that arises when introducing new ideas or practices, including differentiated instruction. It is important to address this resistance to ensure that professional development is successful and effective.

There are several reasons why educators may resist change, such as fear of failure, lack of understanding of the benefits of differentiated instruction, or concern about the additional workload that may come with implementing new teaching methods. To address these concerns, it is important to provide educators with the support and resources they need to feel confident in their ability to implement differentiated instruction.

One effective strategy is to involve educators in the planning and implementation of professional development opportunities. This can help to build buy-in and ownership of the changes being made, as well as provide educators with a sense of control over the process. Encouraging educators to share their concerns and ideas for how to address them can help to foster a collaborative approach to change.

Another strategy is to provide ongoing support and coaching to educators as they implement differentiated instruction in their classrooms. This can include observation and feedback from administrators or instructional coaches, as well as opportunities for educators to collaborate and share best practices with one another.

It is also important to recognize and celebrate the successes that educators achieve in implementing differentiated instruction. This can help to build momentum and enthusiasm for the practice, as well as reinforce the idea that the effort put into making changes is worthwhile.

Overall, addressing resistance to change in professional development for differentiated instruction requires a collaborative and supportive approach that emphasizes the benefits of the practice, provides ongoing support and resources, and celebrates successes along the way.

CHAPTER 15

CONCLUSION

MOVING FORWARD WITH DIFFERENTIATED INSTRUCTION

As educators, it is our responsibility to ensure that all students have access to a high-quality education that meets their individual needs. Differentiated instruction is an essential approach to teaching that allows us to do just that. By tailoring instruction to meet the unique learning needs of each student, we can help all learners achieve academic success and reach their full potential.

However, even with the best intentions, there are ongoing challenges and obstacles to implementing differentiated instruction. In this chapter, we will discuss the importance of continuing to differentiate instruction for diverse learners, address some of the ongoing challenges and obstacles, and provide strategies for moving forward with differentiated instruction.

The Importance of Continuing to Differentiate Instruction for Diverse Learners

Every student has unique strengths, needs, and interests, and it is essential that we continue to differentiate instruction to meet these individual needs. By recognizing and accommodating the diverse backgrounds and experiences of our students, we can create a learning environment that is inclusive, engaging, and supportive of all learners.

Moreover, differentiated instruction has been shown to improve student achievement and motivation, reduce behavior problems, and increase student engagement. Research has also found that students who receive differentiated instruction are more likely to develop critical thinking and problem-solving skills, have a positive attitude toward learning, and show greater retention of material.

Addressing Ongoing Challenges and Obstacles

Despite the many benefits of differentiated instruction, there are ongoing challenges and obstacles to implementing this approach in the classroom. Some of the most common challenges include:

Time constraints: Teachers often struggle to find the time to plan and implement differentiated instruction, particularly when faced with large class sizes and limited resources.

Resistance to change: Some educators may be hesitant to adopt new teaching practices or may feel that differentiated instruction is too complex or difficult to implement.

Lack of support: Teachers may not have access to the necessary resources, such as professional development opportunities or instructional materials, to effectively implement differentiated instruction.

Assessment limitations: Traditional assessments may not accurately measure the learning outcomes of students who receive differentiated instruction, making it difficult to demonstrate the effectiveness of this approach.

Strategies for Moving Forward with Differentiated Instruction

To overcome these challenges and obstacles, educators can employ several strategies to promote and sustain differentiated instruction:

Provide ongoing professional development: Teachers need regular opportunities to learn about and practice differentiated instruction strategies. Professional development can take many forms, including workshops, conferences, coaching, and online courses.

Create a collaborative culture: Collaboration among teachers, administrators, specialists, and parents is essential for effective differentiated instruction. Educators should seek opportunities to work together to share resources, develop instructional materials, and provide feedback on student progress.

Use technology: Technology can be a powerful tool for differentiating instruction. Educators can use online resources, educational apps, and digital tools to provide students with personalized learning experiences and to monitor student progress.

Make time for planning: Teachers must have dedicated planning time to develop and implement differentiated instruction strategies. Administrators can help by providing teachers with common planning time and by creating a schedule that allows for adequate preparation.

Monitor and assess student progress: Regular assessment and monitoring of student progress are critical to determine the effectiveness of differentiated instruction. Teachers should use a variety of assessment strategies to measure student learning outcomes and adjust instruction as necessary.

Differentiated instruction is a powerful approach to teaching that can help us meet the needs of all students. By recognizing the diverse learning needs of our students and adapting instruction accordingly, we can create a learning environment that is engaging, supportive, and inclusive. While there are ongoing challenges and obstacles to implementing differentiated instruction, with the right strategies and support, we can continue to move forward and ensure that all students receive the education they deserve.

www.ingramcontent.com/pod-product-compliance
Lightning Source LLC
Chambersburg PA
CBHW071343090426
42738CB00012B/2998